Lord,
Teach Us
to Pray

Lord, Teach Us to Pray

A Guide to the Spiritual Life
and Christian Discipleship

FR. JEFFREY KIRBY, STL

SAINT BENEDICT+PRESS
Charlotte, North Carolina

Cover design by Caroline Kiser

Front cover image: Icon in St. Stephen's Bulgarian church (photo)/ Godong / UIG / The Bridgeman Art Library

Cataloging-in-Publication data on file with the Library of Congress.

ISBN: 978-1-61890-614-4

Published in the United States by
Saint Benedict Press, LLC
P.O. Box 410487
Charlotte, NC 28241
www.SaintBenedictPress.com

Printed and bound in the United States of America

To

The Men of the Drexel House
Charleston, South Carolina

Contents

PART ONE: "LORD"

PART TWO: "TEACH US"

PART THREE: "TO PRAY"

Foreword

For the Christian, everything flows from discipleship in the Lord Jesus—which is to say that Jesus *calls* us to be his disciples—which is to say that he desires that we follow him and live his Way—which is to say that everything in a Christian's life is a response to Jesus—which is to say that he sends us the Holy Spirit to make us wise in his Way and keep us faithful to him—which is to say that he wishes to use us as his instruments—which is to say that he desires to have a deep, life-long relationship with us— which is to say that he loves us more than we can possibly imagine—which is to say that his love for us eternal, and that he desires that we spend eternity with and in him.

Those words are a mouthful, but they summarize the richness of discipleship and the eternal destiny for which God has made every person. Our discipleship and destiny in Christ form the core of our lives as Christians and should be reflected in everything we do. Though that may seem like a tall, even impossible, order, the Lord has left us the Church, through which we will be schooled and formed in all that he desires. Through the Church, the Lord himself, in the power of the Holy Spirit, will guide, teach, forgive, heal, cleanse, and share his joy. He gives us everything we need to attain that to which he calls us. In fact, it is he who accomplishes it in us! What he asks is that we *follow* him and *cooperate* with his grace.

I have always been intrigued by the passage in Matthew's gospel where Peter quarrels with Jesus about what his mission from the Father will entail. Jesus has revealed to his disciples that he must go to Jerusalem to suffer, die and rise from the dead; but this makes no sense to Peter, who wants a different kind of Messiah, a different path to salvation. Taking Jesus aside, he argues,

> "God forbid, Lord! This shall never happen to you."
> But he turned said to Peter, "Get behind me, Satan! You are a hindrance to me; for you are not on the side of God, but of men" (Mt 16:22–23)

Peter's argument against Jesus' cross and resurrection exposes the fact that he is not *following* but wants to create his own path, one that makes sense to him. He would prefer that Jesus follow *his* way, *his* rationale, *his* plan for salvation. Jesus knows that if Peter is trying to convince him of another way, Peter will never follow him. Thus, he says, "Get behind me." In other words, "Follow me." In another place, Jesus asks his disciples a haunting question: "Why do you call me 'Lord, Lord,' and do not do what I tell you?'" Every disciple must learn to live a life that is compatible with the Lordship of Jesus.

In *Lord, Teach Us to Pray: A Teaching on the Spiritual Life and Discipleship*, Father Jeffrey Kirby lays out the foundations of discipleship and the steps which lead to faithfulness, prayerfulness, hopefulness, conversion of life, and intimate communion with God. One could not possibly aspire to faithful discipleship without a commitment to prayer, and Father Kirby teaches us to pray, just as Jesus taught his first disciples to pray.

Faith issues forth in a desire to know God better, and God leads us as trusted friends to a mature life of Christian love. Prayer increases our faith and deepens our friendship with God, who accomplishes all of this within us. After all, it was God who called us in the first place, God whose love is always first, God who created us to rest in him for all eternity. Along the way of discipleship, he helps us know him and ourselves better. He reveals our faults in the healing context of his mercy. He forgives us and teaches us to be merciful ourselves. He feeds us with his Word and with the Body and Blood of his Son. He helps us set aright the priorities of our lives, so that seeking his kingdom first, "all these things shall be yours as well" (Mt 6:33). He reminds us that as disciples of the One sent by the Father, we are sent by the Son as ambassadors of his unsurpassable truth, instruments of his unfathomable love, reconcilers of the estranged, peacemakers in the midst of conflict, and people of prayer who are grounded in friendship with the Father, through the Son, in the unity of the Holy Spirit.

It is Christ who calls disciples, Christ who forms them, Christ who sends them. And prayer is the way to develop a relationship with him so profound that it strengthens and motivates all we are and do. How could we not communicate daily, honestly, and humbly in prayer with the One who desires with all his heart to teach us to pray and holds us closely as his beloved disciples?

This is a book to inspire, teach, and lead in the Way

who is Jesus. Father Kirby is a wise and clear teacher, and he helps us appreciate the Church's storied tradition of prayer. In doing so, he makes us hunger for more—which is to say, he makes us hunger more for Jesus.

—Archbishop J. Peter Sartain

Introduction

An Amazing Journey

There is nothing in this life more fulfilling or exciting than to follow the Lord Jesus Christ, and there is nothing bolder in this world than to declare that Jesus Christ is Lord and to live the radical adventure of a Christian believer. This is the singular inspiration of this book.

In writing this book, I have drawn from my own discipleship and priesthood, as well as my vocations ministry. As I have led men and women in their discipleship and spiritual life in order to find God's will in their lives, I have learned and collected lived wisdom and practical applications of what it means to live as a Catholic Christian in our contemporary world. I pray that you find this book helpful as you seek to live the amazing journey of being a friend and disciple of the Lord Jesus.

Anxiety and Peace

It was the celebration of my first Mass as a newly ordained priest, and I was very nervous. I wanted everything to go smoothly and, more importantly, I wanted to make sure that I didn't make any mistakes.

As I looked out in the congregation from the presider's chair for the first time, I saw my parents and siblings, nieces and nephews, multiple other family members (some of whom I hadn't seen in years), friends from all the different parts of my life: high school, college, graduate school, and seminary, as well as former co-workers, parishioners from summer assignments, and an array of parishioners from my home parish. It seemed like my whole life was before me. I was joyful but very nervous.

As I concluded the opening Collect and sat down, I was relieved that the first part of the Mass had gone well. I found myself thinking ahead and worrying about the next few parts of the Mass. I allowed a lot of distractions to take over, and I missed a lot of the readings. After we stood for the Alleluia and I gave my first blessing to a deacon to proclaim the Gospel, I was still nervous.

Once I heard the beginning of the Gospel reading, however, I felt a tremendous peace. I had read the Gospel beforehand, but the first verse of the passage powerfully struck me at that moment. It was the beginning of the Eleventh Chapter of St. Luke's Gospel, the petition of the apostles to the Lord Jesus: "Lord, teach us to pray."

After hearing that petition, a great calm came over me. I stopped worrying and let myself enjoy the Mass. I even laughed internally when I thought, "Well, if I make some mistakes, it'll just give people something to talk about!" In hearing the request of the apostles, I heard the deepest request within my own heart being uttered to the Lord: "Lord, teach me to pray." I was getting caught up in all kinds of minutiae and control, anxiety, and fear.

"Lord, teach us to pray" was the simple, heartfelt request that broke through all those heavy anxieties, and was the core of what I wanted at that first Mass.

I repeated that petition to myself as the Mass moved along, and I asked the Lord's help to be a better disciple. I prayed:

- Lord, help me to believe and see your presence and providence in my life and in my ministry;

- Lord, teach me to follow you and to seek the virtues that will help me to be like you;

- Lord, give me a prayerful spirit and the gift of a strong spiritual life.

Our World Today

My personal story applies to this book. In a small way it reflects much of what is happening in our world today.

We live in an amazing time, and in a world with tremendous blessings. Although it is a world marked by anxieties and a restless spirit, it is also a world of questions and of exploration for answers and direction. People are looking for answers. Where are they looking? What do people want to know?

People want to know who God is and they want to know about themselves, about life and its mysteries, and about the afterlife and its truths. At times, however, our world is distracted by its own ego, nervousness, fears, and desire for control. People can lose focus, and indifference or despair can set in. Where can the world turn? Who has the answers?

If humanity turns only to itself or to false prophets, then its inquiry continues with incomplete or wayward guidance, and it leads to journeys without end, to questions without answers, and to a life without meaning.

Jesus, however, enters humanity's state of affairs, and he desires to walk with us. He wants a personal relationship with each one of us, and wishes to be our companion and confidant. The Lord Jesus, who cried human tears, worked with human hands, and loved with a human heart, wants to be with each of us. He co-experiences our sufferings, disappointments, and confusion, as well as our triumphs, joys, and peace. The Lord is with us. He hears our concerns and experiences our trials. He knows each of us better than we know ourselves, and he proposes new and eternal answers to our questions. He announces the Good News and promises an abundant life to those who follow him. The Lord calls each of us out of ourselves and into a deep relationship with him. He waits for a response, for us to accept his invitation to teach us and make us fit for the kingdom of God.

This was the invitation accepted by the apostles. They followed the Lord, lived with him, watched him, ate with him, ministered with him, and sought to find the answers to their questions in his life and teachings. After spending some time with the Lord, the apostles noticed that he secluded himself every evening and spent time in communion and prayer with God the Father. The apostles also knew that St. John the Baptist had taught his disciples how to pray. Motivated by these examples, the apostles approached the Lord one evening after he returned from his solitude and prayer. They asked him simply, "Lord, teach us to pray." They wanted to follow him, and so they humbled themselves and asked him to teach them. This encounter between Christ and the apostles and the apostles' request manifest three very important lessons about the spiritual life:

- The spiritual life is about being in a relationship with God. We address and desire communion with a personal God. It is not simply a random exploration in transcendence or an unguided search into existentialism;

- We cannot give ourselves all that we desire in the spiritual life. We see the depth and richness of the spiritual life, and we must also recognize our interior poverty and helplessness;

- We must be taught. We do not have what we need. We have to accept the humble posture of a person who does not know, and allow God and others to instruct us in the spiritual life.

And so, like the apostles, we have to welcome the Lord into our lives. We have to accept him as our Lord, Teacher, Healer, Friend, Companion, Confidant, our Everything.

We have to become disciples and turn to him, who is the Answer to all our human longings, and ask him, "Lord, teach us to pray." In making this petition, we begin to find in the Lord Jesus all the peace, hope, and joy we seek in our lives.

Why This Book?

In preparing to write this book, and working to collect and present the different portions of the Church's spiritual tradition, I thought often of my first Mass and of that Gospel verse: "Lord, teach us to pray." The verse serves as a great outline for presenting the spiritual wisdom of the Church, since in this concise verse there are three distinct parts: "LORD," "TEACH US," and "TO PRAY."

We'll use these three parts as the three parts of our book. Each part of the book will have three chapters, and will be guided by a question posed by the Lord Jesus in his public ministry. The three parts will present the fundamental aspects of the Church's spiritual tradition, and the dynamic nature between the three parts. Living a life in Jesus Christ will be demonstrated and explained.

- In Part One, we will address Jesus
  Christ as "Lord." We will emphasize
  the need for a life of faith and discipleship. We will be guided by the Lord's
  question: "Who do you say that I am?"
  (Mt 16:15), and will explore the identity of Jesus Christ and his summons
  to each of us. The first part will stress

Baptism and our need for a personal relationship with Jesus Christ. It will address the Eucharist as the heart of our discipleship, and show the Church as a community of faith.

- In Part Two, we will cover our petition to the Lord Jesus to "Teach Us." We will stress the important aspects of conversion and virtue in the life of a Christian disciple. This part of the book will be guided by the Lord's question: "Why do you call me 'Lord, Lord,' and not do what I tell you?" (Lk 6:46), and will define and explain the purgative way, God's law, virtue, and the Rule of Life.

- In Part Three, we will develop our request of the Lord to teach us how "To Pray." We will highlight the universal call to holiness and the different understandings of prayer. We will be guided by the Lord's question: "What do you want me to do for you?" (Lk 18:41). We will address the utter importance of the Eucharist, and provide practical counsels on how to begin or deepen a time of prayer, how to persevere in prayer, and how to sanctify our daily activities in Jesus Christ.

In our spiritual tradition, there are many volumes on the life of prayer and spirituality. Oftentimes, these books are long, incomplete, and heavy. Some books deal extremely well with prayer, but do not address the life of faith and discipleship that is necessary in order to pray in Christ. Other books do not explain conversion or virtue. They neglect the moral life as an essential part of the spiritual life and the workings of God's grace. A person cannot have a relationship with God or a life of authentic prayer if he is not seeking to be like Christ in his actions and behavior. Other books address the life of prayer or aspects of the spiritual life, but do not fully address the practical, tangible aspects of how to pray or grow in virtue.

In addressing all three of these areas, the book intends to be a resource and a guide to Christian disciples who wish to grow in their relationship with the Lord. It is meant to help the reader as both a workshop and a laboratory, offering practical counsel on how to develop a relationship with God: to be with the Lord and let ourselves be loved by him. This book was written and designed as a blueprint and toolbox for the person who truly "hungers and thirsts for righteousness" (Mt 5:6), and who is willing to labor to receive the Lord's blessing on his efforts (Ps 127:1).

PART ONE

"But who do you say that I am?"
Matthew 16:15

"LORD"

CHAPTER ONE

Baptism and a Personal Decision for Christ

"Jesus Christ is Lord!"
Philippians 2:11

Starting the Journey

What a great adventure it is to be a Christian! Throughout the Gospels, we see the apostles and disciples being led and formed by the Lord Jesus in his public ministry. They witnessed his powerful preaching and wondrous signs. We can imagine that the apostles woke up every morning wondering, "What is the Master going to do today?" It was always an adventure, and always led the apostles to follow paths that they would not have taken by themselves. This is the adventure that Jesus offers to us: to join in this life as his friends and disciples.

After following and living with the Lord for some time, Jesus sent out the apostles (the word "apostle" even means "one who is sent") to go and preach the Good News. They were sent out in pairs, and they taught and worked great signs in the Lord's name. After their mission, the apostles reassembled with Jesus in Caesarea-Philippi. After the initial excitement and exchange of stories among the group, the Lord asked a simple question, "Who do men say that the Son of Man is?" It was an easy question: much like delivering the news, and the apostles responded, "John the Baptist," "Elijah," "Jeremiah," and "One of the prophets." It is a question that has echoed through the ages, and many other answers have been reported: "Great Teacher," "Miracle-Worker," "Inspiring Revolutionary."

Jesus then asked the apostles a dramatically more provocative question: "Who do you say that I am?" We can imagine that the festive and relaxed mood of the occasion came to an abrupt end, and suddenly the apostles found themselves with a pressing question that calls for an answer.

The Lord's question given at Caesarea-Philippi is the inspiration and the basis of the first part of our book. In the course of the next three chapters, we will dive into this question and see the answers given by others, and prepare ourselves to give our own answer to the Lord's persistent question: "Who do you say that I am?"

The Human Person

As we begin to reflect on the question that has been given to us by the Lord, we realize how deeply the question resonates within us. Every human person consists of both a body and soul. Just as our body needs things to survive and grow, such as oxygen, water, food, etc., so our soul needs things as well, such as faith, hope, and love. These spiritual longings point to the truth that every human person has a natural desire for God. The human person is a spiritual person, and we all interiorly desire the relationship that God offers to us. In our lives and in our culture, we can find several apparent goods to try and fill the *capax Dei,* which is our capacity for God, oftentimes simply called the "God hole" within us. But, try as we might to fill it with other things, this interior desire can only be completely fulfilled by a relationship with God, and by acts of religion that bind us to him.[1]

There is a story about four young Catholic men who were backpacking through Europe after college graduation. The four agreed to attend Sunday Mass and to pray together every evening on their trek. On one occasion, the group was at a hostel in northern Italy and an Englishman at the hostel noticed them praying. Later he asked them, "So, you all are religious?" One of the group members responded, "Yes, just like you." The gentleman was caught off-guard and protested, "I'm not religious!" To which another group member responded, "Yes, yes you are. You just choose not to exercise your religious nature. I have a muscle here on my arm just like everyone else. You can see the muscle on my arm because I've been backpacking and it's conditioned. Everyone else has this muscle, but perhaps it can't be seen on them because they haven't exercised it. In the same way, yes, we're all religious. We're just trying to exercise it." The group explained it well. We are all spiritual and religious persons. Will we exercise this part of our personhood?

In these observations of our human nature, it is

---

1   *Catechism of the Catholic Church,* #27-30.

helpful to be reminded that we were all made by God and for God, and that he never ceases to draw us to himself. The Lord Jesus invites us and welcomes us to be with him. He asks each of us: "Who do you say that I am?"

A Response Is Needed

In our world today, we see an incredible openness to God and to religious sentiment. These noble inquiries are good and need affirmation. They also need direction. Like ancient Athens, there are many religious monuments throughout the Mars Hill of today (cf. Acts 17:16–34). Once again, in the midst of so many monuments and religious opinions, the Good News is proclaimed. As St. Paul did over two thousand years ago, the Church once again raises up the Person of Jesus Christ and offers him as the answer to all of humanity's needs, hopes, and aspirations. Once again the reality of God becoming a man, suffering, dying, and rising from the dead, and again offering us his friendship, is announced and extended to each of us. In our spinning world, the steadfastness of the Cross and Resurrection are boldly announced, fear flees, and true friendship with God is offered to us.

And so, the Lord Jesus asks us: "Who do you say that I am?" The invitation endures. The question is a tremendously important one, since it lies at the heart of our desire to learn about prayer. The spiritual life is a relationship with God. If we desire a relationship with someone, we have to know who they are. We can only love what we know; therefore we have to come to know who Jesus Christ is in our lives. In addition, our answer to the Lord's question determines our level of surrender, trust, docility, and the reception we give to his teachings. The answer we give to the Lord's question will determine whether we accept the Lord's invitation to be in a relationship with him.

Some people answer the Lord's question indirectly or incompletely. They note that they have heard about Jesus, are curious about his miracles, are inspired by his teachings, or revere his historical legacy. Some will answer that Jesus is a great teacher, a miracle-worker, or an inspiring revolutionary. While each of these responses could be good in themselves, each of them is based on actions and functions, and none of them deal with a true relationship marked by a desire to be with the Lord. These responses do not accept the intimacy that the Lord Jesus offers us. Each of these responses, and ones similar to them, are incomplete and limit our compliance to the Lord Jesus and his way of life. People only trust a teacher in the areas of their lives where they feel instruction is needed; people only watch a miracle-worker for entertainment or because they want something; and people only follow a revolutionary because they want a structure or ideology challenged and overthrown. Each of these are limited, and do not establish a deep relationship. Additionally, beyond these answers themselves, we have to acknowledge that this supposed good teacher, miracle worker, and revolutionary claimed, in fact, to be God. The implications of this claim are huge. As C. S. Lewis put it: Jesus is either Lord, a Liar, or a Lunatic.[2]

---

2   C. S. Lewis, *Mere Christianity,* Book II, Chapter 3.

- Jesus is Lord as he understood himself and as he truly is;

- Or Jesus is a Liar since he claimed to be God and knew that he was not;

- Or he is a Lunatic since he believed he was God but is not the Lord in reality.

This three-point summary deconstructs many supposed answers that seek the middle ground: "I respect the teachings of Jesus and try to live by them and be a good person," or, "I accept the contribution that Jesus has made to spiritual wisdom and I find his teachings inspiring along with the teachings of several others." These types of answers try to absorb Jesus of Nazareth into a broad conglomerate of recognized spiritual teachers, and they avoid Jesus' direct question: "Who do you say that I am?" Will we avoid generalized answers and understand the singular and utter importance of our answer to this question? Will we understand how much is at stake for us in our answer to this question? How will we answer? Who is Jesus to us?

Baptismal Dignity

In acknowledging the Lord's question and seeing our natural state as human beings who have a desire for God, it is also extremely important that we remind ourselves of our spiritual state. Principally, we must not diminish or forget the primacy of our Baptism. We must come to a greater understanding that our relationship with God begins with baptism, the initial sacrament of Christian life and faith.[3]

Oftentimes when Christian believers are asked why Baptism is necessary, they respond that it is necessary so that original sin (and any actual sins) might be removed from the person's soul. This is indeed true, but not complete. Why is sin removed? Why is this important? It is important because as the Lord Jesus removes our sin in Baptism, we enter into a covenant with God. We are incorporated into the Body of Christ, which is the Church. We now participate and are called to re-live the Lord's Paschal Mystery—his passion, death, and resurrection—in our daily lives. God the Father accepts us, is well pleased with us, and makes us members of his own family. We become temples of the Holy Spirit. Sin is removed at Baptism so that these greater, divine actions can occur within us. Baptism is truly our adoption ceremony into the life of the Holy Trinity—Father, Son, and Holy Spirit—and into the living household of faith. We are blessed with God's presence in our very selves, and are endowed with the theological virtues of faith, hope, and charity.[4]

Baptismal Way of Life

Since we are baptized Christians and live as members of Christ's Body, we are called to re-live the Paschal Mystery.

---

3   *Catechism of the Catholic Church*, 1213, 1253.
4   *Catechism of the Catholic Church*, #1268-1269, 1279.

As the Lord Jesus died and rose again, we are called to die
to ourselves and our sinfulness, and to live in him and
seek to follow him in all our ways.[5]

St. Paul juxtaposes two ways of life, and labels them
as "life according to the flesh" (with "flesh" meaning our
fallen attraction to evil and pleasure, and not necessarily
our bodies), and "life according to the Spirit" (Rom 8:3–
13). In order for us to live in Christ and follow a life in the
Spirit, we have to truly die to ourselves and our sinfulness, and seek to live according to the person and teachings of the Lord Jesus.[6] As St. Paul asked the Christians in
ancient Rome, so he asks us:

> Do you not know that all of us who have been bap-
> tized into Christ Jesus were baptized into his death?
> We were buried therefore with him by baptism into
> death, so that as Christ was raised from the dead by
> the glory of the Father, we too might walk in new-
> ness of life (Rom 6:3–4).

What does this mean?

Imagine if you and some of your closest friends were
on a large boat on a nice lake. You were all relaxed enjoy-
ing the gentle movement of the boat and a cold drink,
when all of a sudden you heard a noise in the water
behind you. You can tell from the faces of the people in
front of you who can see behind you that something is
not right. Something suddenly grabs you from behind
and throws you over the boat. Splash! You hit the water

---

5 *Catechism of the Catholic Church*, #1691, 1694-1697.
6 *Catechism of the Catholic Church*, #628, 1227-1228.

and are fighting to break free. You sink deeper into the water, and you can see the boat getting farther and farther away from you. You are wrestling to break free. As you are able to look behind you, you're shocked when you realize that it is actually Jesus who is holding you. You scream from within, "Lord, let me go, I'm drowning. I'm dying. Let me go!" Welcome to the waters of Baptism! It is only when we are willing to die to ourselves in Christ that we are able to live in him and be born to newness of life.

Pope Saint John Paul II teaches this very truth in his first encyclical, *Redeemer of Man*:

> The man who wishes to understand himself thoroughly—and not just in accordance with immediate, partial, often superficial, and even illusory standards and measures of his being—he must with his unrest, uncertainty, and even his weakness and sinfulness, with his life and death, draw near to Christ. He must, so to speak, enter into him with all his own self, he must 'appropriate' and assimilate the whole of the reality of the Incarnation and Redemption in order to find himself.[7]

This way of life is clearly taught and expressed in the Baptismal Promises. In the first three promises we denounce sin, the wayward attraction to sin, and Satan. In the last three promises we acknowledge the array of Christian beliefs, assert our faith in the Holy Trinity and in Jesus Christ, and acknowledge the Church. Seen here,

---

7   John Paul II, *Redeemer of Man*, #10.

the baptismal promises fully summarize the biblical and constant teaching on the baptismal way of life of the Christian believer:

Do you renounce sin, so as to live in the freedom of the children of God?

Do you reject the lure of evil, so that sin may have no mastery over you?

Do you reject Satan, the author and prince of sin?

Do you believe in God, the Father almighty, creator of heaven and earth?

Do you believe in Jesus Christ, his only Son, our Lord, who was born of the Virgin Mary, suffered death and was buried, rose again from the dead, and is seated at the right hand of the Father?

Do you believe in the Holy Spirit, the Holy Catholic Church, the communion of saints, the forgiveness of sins, the resurrection of the body, and life everlasting?[8]

Faith and Baptism

As we understand our Baptism and review the promises of this first sacrament, we begin to deepen our comprehension of what it means to be a member of the family of God. We perceive anew why it is important to have a relationship with the Lord Jesus, and we start to grasp the context from which the Lord's question—"Who do you say that I

---

8   *Roman Catholic Missal*, Easter Vigil Mass.

am?"—is given and why our answer is so important.

The grace of faith is poured into us at baptism, and yet some initial faith is needed in order to be baptized. Those of us who were baptized as children had our parents attest to their own faith, a type of "proxy faith" for us, and they pledged that they would raise us in the faith. Those who were baptized as adults went through a catechumenate (usually the Rite of Christian Initiation of Adults [RCIA]) and had their initial faith formed so that they could receive Baptism. At Baptism itself, however, a tremendous outpouring of faith was given to each of us. If we're not careful, this grace can sit in our souls and never fully be used. Sadly, in many Christians, the faith that is called forth from the baptized is never fully accepted, integrated, and lived out.[9] How can we grow into our Baptism? What is faith?

The author of the Letter to the Hebrews writes that "faith is the assurance of things hoped for, the conviction of things not seen" (Heb 11:1). Two words that stand out in this explanation are "assurance" and "conviction," and Pope St. John Paul II continues in that spirit in his encyclical, *Splendor of Truth*:

> Faith is a decision involving one's whole existence.
> It is an encounter, a dialogue, a communion of love
> and life between the believer and Jesus Christ, the
> Way, and the Truth, and the Life (cf. Jn 14:6). It
> entails an act of trusting abandonment to Christ,
> which enables us to live as he lived (cf. Gal 2:20),

---

9   *Catechism of the Catholic Church*, #1231, 1247-1255.

in profound love of God and of our brothers and sisters.[10]

How do we live by faith? Following the example and counsel of St. Paul, we have to "rekindle the gift of God" that we have received. We are called to realize what we have been given in Baptism, to seek ways to grow in our faith, to make a personal decision for Jesus Christ and boldly answer the Lord's question: "Who do you say that I am?"

Pope St. John Paul II teaches us in the encyclical *Mission of the Redeemer*:

> From the outset, conversion is expressed in faith which is total and radical, and which neither limits nor hinders God's gift. At the same time, it gives rise to a dynamic and lifelong process which demands a continual turning away from "life according to the flesh" to "life according to the Spirit" (cf. Rom 8:3–13). Conversion means accepting, by a personal decision, the saving sovereignty of Christ and becoming his disciple.[11]

St. Paul of Tarsus

As we grow in our understanding of Christian Baptism and the role of formation in making a personal decision for Christ, and as we seek to answer the Lord's question, it might be helpful for us to look at a great witness from the Sacred Scriptures.

---

10   John Paul II, *Splendor of Truth*, #88.
11   John Paul II, *Mission of the Redeemer*, #46.

In the years after Jesus' death and Resurrection, Saul of Tarsus was a fierce persecutor of the Christian community and a man who was feared by believers: "Saul laid waste to the Church, entered house after house, dragged off men and women and committed them to prison" (Acts 8:3). After persecuting the Church in Jerusalem, Saul was "still breathing threats and murder against the disciples of the Lord" and asked for letters to go to Damascus and search for any Christians (Acts 9:1–2). On his way to the city, "a light from heaven flashed about him," and a voice said to him, "Saul, Saul, why do you persecute me?" When Saul asked who it was, the voice responded, "I am Jesus, whom you are persecuting" (Acts 9:4–5). After this encounter with the Lord, Saul was blinded and did not eat for three days. God sent Ananias to Saul. Ananias laid hands on him, healed him, and then gave him Baptism. After being baptized, Saul ate again and was made strong (Acts 9:17–19).

After accepting the graces of conversion and being baptized, Saul realized that he needed time with the Lord and formation in the Christian way of life. He went and spent some time in the desert of Arabia (Gal 1:17), and then sought out St. Peter and sat at his feet for instruction for fifteen days (Gal 1:18). One can only imagine the humility of Saul. He was one of the most educated men of his day, a student of the great Rabbi Gamaliel and a Roman citizen, and he sought instruction from a Galilean fisherman. Saul knew he needed formation, and he sought guidance and direction.

Rekindling the gift he received from God at Baptism,

and nurtured by his prayer and instruction, Saul—who decided to be called by his Roman name Paul after his conversion—was able to make his personal decision for Christ. In answer to the Lord's question, "Who do you say that I am?" St. Paul boldly declared that "Jesus Christ is Lord" (Phil 2:11). He understood the full depth of that declaration in his life, as he wrote:

> I have been crucified with Christ; it is no longer I who live, but Christ who lives in me; and the life I now live in the flesh I live by faith in the Son of God, who loved me and gave himself for me. (Gal 2:20)

An Enduring Invitation

In seeing the witness of St. Paul, we need to remind ourselves that each of us is invited to encounter Jesus of Nazareth and that each of us is given an invitation to accept him as Lord and Messiah. Jesus chooses us and offers us the powerful opportunity to enter into a loving relationship with him (cf. Jn 15:16). We are offered his friendship, even as he manifests his friendship to us (cf. 1 Jn 3:16, 4:19). The Lord asks us the pressing question: "Who do you say that I am?" The answer to this essential question is the determining factor of where the Lord's invitation will go in our lives, and whether the door of faith will continue to be opened to us.

Will we accept Jesus as Lord? Will we humble ourselves and accept him as the Lord of our lives, and live as his friends and disciples?

CHAPTER TWO

Jesus Christ and Salvation History

"My Lord and My God."
John 20:28

A New Horizon

As we continue through Part One, we continue to hear the question given to us by the Lord Jesus: "Who do you say that I am?" In the last chapter, we reviewed the role of Baptism and the importance of making a personal decision for the Lord Jesus. In this chapter, inspired by the depth and breadth of the baptismal promises, we'll place the declaration of "Jesus as Lord" within the broad context of the Holy Trinity, salvation history and its covenants, and the development of a true relationship with the Lord Jesus in the midst of this new and magnificent horizon.

One Response Leads to Another

To see the full scope of the relationship into which the Lord is inviting us, we have to start with a simple truth: God is real. Yes, it is truly that simple. We have to begin with the assertion that God is real so we can begin to understand his initiative and desire to be in a relationship with us.

Two witnesses to this basic truth might help us.

Some years ago, the Catholic high school in Charleston, South Carolina, received an amazing grace when one of its star students and former homecoming queen decided to answer a call to religious life and enter the convent. People were legitimately surprised and asked all sorts of questions. The world was at the fingertips of this young woman, and she chose to give everything to God—but why?

Another story: Several years ago, a young man who was a senior at a South Carolina college joined a discernment group to help determine God's will for his life. As the young man began to grow in his relationship with God, in prayer, and in virtue, he began to hear a call that he was not expecting. Suddenly Africa kept coming to him in prayer. He had never been to Africa and he didn't know what it meant. Through some of the Church's missionary societies, he was able to visit West Africa for a couple of weeks. When he returned, he spoke about the government corruption, the poverty of the people, the rampant violence, and the lack of clean water and immunizations. He further spoke about the problems with hygiene, nutrition, and malaria. But, after mentioning all these problems and showing his maturity in the spiritual life, this young Christian said that he had never felt more himself, and that he had found his place in life. He knew why he was born. Currently, this young man is single for the Lord and one of our missionaries in West Africa. Why would he give up a regular life? Why would he go to West Africa and risk his safety and health?

Our understanding of God is at the heart of the answer to the questions surrounding these two young people. Unfortunately, some people's understanding of God is that he is a nice fantasy, a cherished heirloom, a psychological consolation, or an entertaining hobby. None of these understandings, however, makes sense of the vows of a religious sister, or the life of a single person in missionary work, or the vows of two married Christian people, or the demands of Christian discipleship in general. These life-altering decisions demand an answer to the question "Who is God?" that goes beyond a mere fantasy or a happy feeling.

We begin to understand the sacrifices we are called to make as Christian disciples if we see God as a real, personal being who has an intimate, self-revealing relationship with humanity. If we understand God as our loving Creator, who knows us better than we know ourselves, we begin to discern that he has a specific plan for each of us. If we comprehend that God is not my creation, or my idea, or even my consolation, then we start to encounter the independent reality of God that compels and sustains our free surrender to his will. As Christian disciples, we begin to see why we are called and willing to surrender our lives to whatever God wants because he is real, he loves us, and his call leads us to fulfillment in this life and to eternal life in heaven.

As a real, personal being, God calls each of us

according to our gifts and talents into an intimate communion with himself. At times, union with God will call
for a loving sacrifice of our own desires and aspirations,
as well as selfless service to others and their needs. This
is what inspired these young Christians, and this is the
conviction that led them to say "yes" to the Lord's call
wherever it led them.

Real People, Real Relationship

It was precisely the truth that "God is real" that was the
source of these young people's surrender and acceptance
of their vocations. If God is not real, if he is merely a creation of our own mind, desires, or fears, then sacrifice
wouldn't make sense; none of us would be able to truly
offer our lives to a fantasy or illusion. Good psychology tells us that we can only have meaningful relation-
ships with "real people." And while this is a psychological
truth, it's also an authentic truth. If someone is only
my "imaginary friend" then that person cannot be my
true friend, and the relationship is as imaginary as the
make-believe friend itself. If we can understand this
basic truth, then we can begin to deepen our comprehension of how important it is that we know that God
is real and that he desires a legitimate relationship with
us. He asks us who we think he is, and then he desires
to teach, correct, heal, and mature our knowledge of
him.[12]

---

12 *Catechism of the Catholic Church*, #205-217.

Changing People? Changing God?

Imagine if someone said they were your friend, but then told people supposedly factual things about you that they knew weren't true. Imagine if this self-proclaimed friend were to regularly and consciously change things about you because they preferred you to have those false qualities. Philosophy would call this "metaphysical confusion" and popular culture would just call it "weird."

There was once an older woman who was a refined socialite, respected by her circle of wealthy and influential friends. Through the woman's involvement in her church, she came to know a talented, young, Hispanic woman. The two became good friends, and the older woman invited the younger woman to a social function. The group was critical of immigration efforts, and when the young woman arrived, they expressed concern over why she was at the party. The older woman, wanting things to go smoothly and not wanting to lose the respect of her friends, told them that the younger women was Italian. When the younger woman heard this she was severely hurt by the lie and left the gathering. The Hispanic woman was offended because who she was as a person was taken from her. She wasn't considered to be good enough or acceptable to the older woman's group of friends. The Hispanic woman was happy with who she was, with her family, and her culture and background. This story highlights the point that real people and their true identity must be acknowledged and respected. That is also true of God. We need to approach God as he truly is and not how we want him to be.

We are real people with a real identity and with true, actual features that reflect who we are. In the same way, God is real, and cannot be changed according to our preferences. Some might say that "God understands" and attempt to justify all sorts of evil or unkindness. Others might say that "God can be whatever you want him to be," but this is an indirect way of saying that God does not truly exist, since real beings have an identity. Saying that God is whatever you want him to be dismisses his real identity and replaces it with our personal interests. This is the beginning of what the Sacred Scriptures call an idol.

If we want to begin to answer the Lord's question— "Who do you say that I am?"—then we have to begin with God as a real, personal being, and not our imaginary friend-god who will be whatever we want him to be. If we want a real relationship with God, we have to acknowledge that he is real. Once we begin to see God's reality, then we can begin to see God as he truly is and as he has revealed himself to be.

"My Lord and My God"

As we accept the Lord's reality and perfect identity, we have to encounter the Lord Jesus and attempt to answer his question to each of us. Perhaps a witness can help us in this process.

After spending three years with the Lord, the apostles witnessed his brutal passion, torture, and crucifixion. Three days later, the apostles received word that Jesus had risen. He then appeared to them and proclaimed the forgiveness of sin and the establishment of peace between

God and humanity. St. Thomas, one of the apostles, was not present during this visit of the Lord. When the other apostles told him, "We have seen the Lord," he did not believe them. He said boldly, "Unless I see in his hands the print of the nails, and place my finger in the mark of the nails, and place my hand in his side, I will not believe." In many ways, St. Thomas reflects our own hesitations and doubts. Is Jesus Christ the Lord? The Resurrection declares this reality, but Thomas was not sure. He wrestled and struggled to make the declaration that Jesus is risen, that Jesus is Lord.

Some days later, the Lord Jesus reappeared to his apostles, and Thomas was present. The Lord once again declared peace and then said to Thomas, "Put your finger here, and see my hands; and put out your hand, and place it in my side; do not be faithless, but believing." St. Thomas saw the risen Lord and knew that Christ was no ghost, but completely real. From this conviction, St. Thomas was able to answer the Lord's question. He found new strength and boldly proclaimed, "My Lord and my God" (Jn 20:28). Thomas was now ready and able to answer the Lord's question. He saw and announced that Jesus was his Lord and God. Jesus replied first to St. Thomas and then to each of us: "You have believed because you have seen me. Blessed are those who have not seen and yet believe." As we have the same question given to us, what will we answer? As we see God's reality, what will be our response to the Lord's question: "Who do you say that I am?"

Like St. Thomas, we are called to accept Jesus as Lord

and God. If we accept his rule of love and enter into a relationship with him, then we accept his invitation in all its fullness and truly become his friends and disciples. The assertion of Jesus as Lord and God is what makes us alive as Christians; it enlivens us to live as "little Christ's" in our world.

By the proclamation of Jesus as Lord and God, we mean that in the Lord Jesus we find the meaning, value, and purpose of our lives and of our world. We surrender to him and see in his person and teachings the perfect guide for our lives. We see in the Lord Jesus our Savior who freed us from sin and from our fallen world. In the Lord Jesus, we see our perfect friend, teacher, healer, confidant, and companion. We see our Everything. This is the response of a disciple.

Personal Relationship with a Real Person

Inspired by St. Thomas, we acknowledge the reality of God and desire to encounter him, as we hear the echo of the Lord's question: "Who do you say that I am?"

We are reminded of Pope Emeritus Benedict XVI who taught us:

> Being a Christian is not the result of an ethical decision or a lofty idea, but the encounter with an event, a person, which gives life a new horizon and a decisive direction.[13]

---

13   Pope Benedict XVI, *God is Love*, #1.

As we desire to comprehend more fully the depth of the question that has been asked of us by the Lord, we hear his summons, "Come to me, all who labor and are heavy laden, and I will give you rest. Take my yoke upon you and learn from me; for I am gentle and lowly in heart, and you will find rest for your souls" (Mt 11:28–29). God, the great "I AM" (Ex 3:14), is also good (Lk 18:19), and is love (1 Jn 4:8). Beyond the perception of intellectual design and the natural sciences, beyond the reflection of the philosophers and the study of existence, we are called to encounter the true God, who is, who is good, and who has chosen us and loves us.

> You did not choose me, but I chose you and appointed you that you should go and bear fruit and that your fruit should abide. (Jn 15:16)

> By this we know love, that he laid down his life for us; and we ought to lay down our lives for the brethren. (1 Jn 3:16)

Realizing the invitation that has been given to us, we come to a greater understanding of the "new horizon" that is before us and that can open up to us if we answer the Lord's question. In wanting to answer the question and live the answer we give, we are immediately led to seek more knowledge of the Lord. We desire to spiritually touch the wounds on his side and probe the nail marks on his hand. We can only love what we know, and so we ask the questions of Jesus that we would ask of any good friend:

- Where does Jesus come from?

- What is his story: his history and background?

- What's his family like?

- What does he do for a living? What are his interests?

Where Jesus Comes From and His Divine Family

As we approach the basic truth that God is real, we are led to ask several very important follow-up questions. If God is real, then how can I come to know him? It's a great question, but a question that leads us to an answer that requires both faith and humility. By ourselves, we cannot know God. In a first grace, God gives us reason that allows us to know some aspects of him. We can discern and recognize that God is all-powerful, all-knowing, and all-good.[14] This is similar to basic knowledge that we might have about a friend: she breathes, is tall, and has a good personality. But that knowledge does not really go to the heart or give us a foundation for friendship. This is also true in our rapport with God. Even such basic knowledge by itself can be difficult to understand in reference to God, and certainly such elementary knowledge is not enough to support a relationship with him. In our friendships, it is our self-disclosure and our friend's

---

14   *Catechism of the Catholic Church*, #31-35.

self-revelation, a mutual sharing of one another's lives which begins and nurtures true friendship. While this can take different forms and expressions according to cultures and different personalities, the unveiling of our hearts is needed for authentic friendship. As this is true in our human friendships, so it is profoundly true in our relationship with God.

In our relationship with God, however, we rely on his initiative. In his relationship with humanity and in his relationship with each one of us, God is the one who invites us and offers the beginning of a relationship. In order to go beyond basic observations about God, we need faith. In making the act of faith, God then reveals himself to us. God shares his own knowledge of himself with us.[15] He is a serious and committed friend, and he calls us to self-reveal ourselves to him and welcome him into our lives as his question stirs in our heart: "Who do you say that I am?"

As God unveils himself to us, we see that he is infinitely perfect in himself and exists as a communion of persons: Father, Son, and Holy Spirit. Perhaps we once thought of God as a distant old man with a long, white beard on a removed throne, but God shows us who he truly is. God reveals to us that in his innermost essence he is not solitude but family. God is a family—a communion—of persons. What does that mean? Why is that important to us?

Realizing that God exists as three persons in a

---

15 *Catechism of the Catholic Church*, #35-38.

relationship of love and self-donation helps us to understand who we are since we are made in God's image (Gn
1:27). This reality further helps us to understand why
God created us and why he is inviting us into a relationship with himself.[16] This is just who God is: he is a communion of persons, a relationship, a divine family. The
Father and the Son love and serve one another, and the
love between them is the Holy Spirit. God is three distinct persons, equal in dignity and majesty, who love one
another.[17]

Jesus' Background and History

In coming to understand God as a family, we have a new
horizon opening up before us and a greater capacity to
see why God is calling us into a relationship with himself.
It helps us to realize that God, who is infinitely perfect
and blessed in himself, truly has a plan of sheer goodness that began when he freely created us, that has been
played out in the course of the ages, and now rests upon
the question of the Lord Jesus: "Who do you say that I
am?" Depending on how we choose to answer that question, we have the opportunity to live in Christ and share
in God's own blessed life.[18] But, what is this plan? How
has it played out? Why is this plan important in understanding Jesus' background and history? How can this
plan help us to answer the Lord's question?

---

16 Catechism of the Catholic Church, #1701-1709.
17 Catechism of the Catholic Church, #234, 240, 253-256.
18 Catechism of the Catholic Church, #1, 50-52.

God's Plan of Sheer Goodness

For us to understand God's plan, we have to begin to grasp that the Holy Trinity does everything together. Each person has a role to play in every action completed by the Godhead. An easy way to understand this interaction is the simple expression: God the Father through Jesus Christ by the power of the Holy Spirit. In every action taken by the Godhead, this is the exchange: God the Father acts, he acts through his Son, and always acts by the power of the Holy Spirit. One person of the Holy Trinity never acts alone. It is always a shared action done in communion between the three persons of the Godhead. It is good for us to remember this interaction between the Father, Son, and Holy Spirit as we try to understand God's plan of sheer goodness toward us.[19] With this in mind, how can we begin to understand God's plan?

In his public preaching, the Lord Jesus recounted a story of a woman who lost a treasured coin. The woman cleared the entire house, dusted, and searched high and low looking for the coin. She moved furniture, adjusted belongings; she was energetic and single-minded in her search for this lost coin. Once she found the coin, she celebrated and called her friends in to rejoice with her (Lk 15:8–10).

This is a great story, and one we can all understand, as we have all searched desperately for lost car keys or a misplaced cell phone or other personal belongings.

---

19   *Catechism of the Catholic Church,* #257-260.

This story is also a great start for us in understanding the "why" of God's plan of salvation. So often today we stress humanity's search for God, but we forget that the great assertion of the Judeo-Christian tradition is that we might search for God, but God desperately searches for us! The story of this woman and the missing coin is a helpful reminder to us, since the woman reflects God himself as he clears the house, moves and adjusts things, searching for lost humanity. God truly desires us to be with him, and he seeks us out and calls us to himself. He looks for the lost coin of our hearts and is willing to dust and clean and do whatever is needed for us to respond well to the Lord's pressing question, "Who do you say that I am?"

As we encounter this amazing mystery of how God searches for us, we can discern the divine pedagogy, the way in which God enlightens, teaches, and forms us to comprehend his words and deeds among us. We recognize that God only gradually reveals himself to us. He prepares us to learn and encounter him by particular stages in a measured plan of salvation. In his wisdom and goodness, God only gradually reveals himself so that we are ready and able to receive the revelation he desires to give us. This is true in the plan of salvation, and this is true in our reception of the divine plan in our own discipleship. God meets us where we are and begins to share his truths and mysteries with us, as we are able to receive them. Then gradually he leads us where we need to be. As God explains his deeds and words to us, we can begin to see how they are intrinsically bound to each other, how each stage sheds light on the other, and how the plan unfolds and becomes clearer to humanity and to each of us.[20]

An example might help us to understand these aspects of God's plan. In many high school biology classes, the students dissect frogs. It was common in old lab books to have one basic picture of just the outline of the frog. Then there were multiple plastic sheets that the student could flip over the frog outline, and each sheet would have a different aspect of the frog that would highlight that particular part while also showing something of the whole frog. So, a student could flip over the plastic sheet on the muscle structure of the frog and see its whole muscle system, or flip over the sheet of the frog's circulatory system and see that bodily system, and so on. Each plastic sheet would show something uniquely its own, but would also build upon, complement, and highlight something of the whole frog. In having all the sheets together, then, the student could see the whole frog. As we understand this basic example, we can understand the stages of God's plan and how each one teaches us something particularly its own, while also developing, enriching, and expanding God's overall revelation, his self-disclosure, to humanity to each one of us. So, what are the stages of God's plan? What does each stage teach us about God? How does God's plan help us to answer the question of the Lord Jesus?

---

20   *Catechism of the Catholic Church,* #51-55.

The Stages of God's Plan

As we review the plan of salvation, we begin with God's loving invitation to humanity, and how we turned away from God and chose other things over him. Our first parents, Adam and Eve, sought their own glory over God's and refused to accept his offer of friendship. This original sin caused a break and division in our love for God and in our relationship with him. Rather than leave us in darkness and despair, God the Father immediately sought reconciliation with us and promised to send a savior and to bestow blessings upon us.

Each of the different stages in God's plan develops the promise of a messiah, an anointed savior, who would come and save us, and restore us to the Father. Each of the subsequent stages would be marked by a covenant and by a further disclosure of God and a broadening of the blessings to greater portions of humanity. Each stage unveils how much God truly loves us, and gives us even more knowledge of who God is. Each stage prepares us more for the fulfillment of God's promise of a savior and of abundant life in him.

The different covenants of the various stages of God's plan are given in the *Catechism of the Catholic Church*, and are best summarized by the mediators of the respective covenants.[21] These mediators can be narrowed down to Adam, Noah, Abraham, Moses, and David. Each of

---

21 *Catechism of the Catholic Church*, #54-64, 2569-2589; cf. Scott Hahn, *A Father Who Keeps His Promises*. St. Anthony Messenger Press, 1998.

them carried the promise of a Messiah and prepared for his coming. Each of them presided over their respective covenants that deepened our knowledge of God and expanded the circle of the recipients of God's blessings. King David's covenant was the grand blueprint of the new and eternal covenant established by the Lord Jesus. In each of the diverse covenants and the stages of revelation they represent, we see the patient working of God and the family history of Jesus Christ.

Mediator and Fullness

This background and history help us to know Jesus and approach him as Lord and Savior, and as the Mediator and Fullness of all God's revelation. In God's plan of sheer goodness, the divine Son, the Second Person of the Holy Trinity, witnessed humanity's fall from grace through original sin and the subsequent actual sins throughout human history. God the Father saw the loss of his created children, and God the Son cried to the Father, "Here am I! Send me" (Is 6:8). In the fullness of time, the Son offered to ransom and redeem the lost children of Adam and Eve. The Second Person of the Godhead became a man in Jesus of Nazareth, and shows us the face of our Heavenly Father.[22] In God becoming a man, we witness in exemplary fashion, that while humanity pines and searches for an "unknown God" (Acts 17:23) "in many and various ways" (Hebrews 1:1), God is the one who desperately searches for humanity. At the beginning of

---

22   *Catechism of the Catholic Church*, #606-609.

this mystery, Zachariah, the father of St. John the Baptist, would exclaim, "the day shall dawn upon us," (Lk 1:78), and St. John rightly sings, "The Word became flesh and dwelt among us" (Jn 1:14), and "Behold, the dwelling of God is with men" (Rev 21:3).

In the beauty of the mystery of God becoming a human being, we hear the question again raised by the Lord Jesus and directed to each of us: "Who do you say that I am?" St. Thomas has responded, "My Lord and my God," and St. Paul has exclaimed, "Jesus Christ is Lord!" What is our answer? What will we say? Who is Jesus Christ to us?

CHAPTER THREE

My Faith—the Church's Faith

"You are the Christ, the Son of the living God."
Matthew 16:16

Back to Caesarea-Philippi

In Part One of our book, we have been focusing on approaching Jesus of Nazareth as "Lord," since any growth in the spiritual life must begin with a relationship with him. We started with the story of Jesus and the apostles, and the Lord's poignant question: "Who do you say that I am?" We have looked at different aspects of this question, and we have heard the testimony of St. Paul that "Jesus Christ is Lord," and from St. Thomas who declared: "My Lord and my God." Now we find ourselves back at Caesarea-Philippi. We can imagine the awkward pause that initially followed the Lord's directed question, until one apostle broke the silence and spoke up. The chief apostle, the one who was always willing to jump (sometimes without looking), St. Peter, declared to Jesus: "You are the Christ, the Son of the living God." As we find ourselves with the Lord, what will be our answer? Will we make a personal decision for Jesus Christ? In our own lives, will we declare that Jesus is Lord?

As members of the baptized, we have received the gift of faith and are called to live as Christians. We continue on the path of a post-baptismal catechumenate, a time of formation and preparation for us to accept and live as friends and disciples of the Lord Jesus. A personal decision for the Lord is needed in our lives. We are called to rekindle the gift that God has given to us, and are invited into a relationship of love that participates and re-lives the Paschal Mystery.[23]

The radical nature of the Lord's question cannot be denied. If we try to avoid a decision for Christ, but continue to live as supposed Christians, as cultural Catholics, then we will slowly compromise the radical nature of the Lord's call. We will be led on an unconscious or disguised program to diminish the person of the Lord Jesus, to secularize his message, and to turn the Gospel into a really bad self-help guidebook. As the Lord himself would challenge us:

> I know your works; you are neither cold nor hot. Would that you were cold or hot! So, because you are lukewarm, and neither cold nor hot, I will spew you out of my mouth. (Rev 3:15–16)

This exhortation should not frighten or intimidate us, but should emphasize and accentuate how utterly important our answer to the Lord's question truly is in our lives and our true discipleship.

---

23 *Catechism of the Catholic Church,* #423-424, 1231, 1428.

Come, Holy Spirit

The personal decision we are called to make for Christ is facilitated and called forth from us by the Holy Spirit, whom we received at Baptism. The Holy Spirit works within us to see God's love, and helps us to follow the Lord Jesus as his friends and disciples (cf. 1 Cor 12:3; Gal 4:6).[24]

When St. Paul first visited Ephesus, after spending some time with the young Christian community there, he realized that something was lacking. He asked the Ephesians: "Did you receive the Holy Spirit when you believed?" They responded, "No, we have never even heard that there is a Holy Spirit" (Acts 19:1–7). Talk about bad catechesis! How did these Christians never hear about the Holy Spirit? Nevertheless, St. Paul laid his hands upon them, and the Holy Spirit came on them.

In our own discipleship, we have also received the Holy Spirit. Did we know that? Do we know who the Holy Spirit is? We received the Holy Spirit at Baptism, but also in a singular way in the sacrament of Confirmation. In this sacrament, the baptized person freely asks a bishop, as a successor of the apostles, to call down the Holy Spirit upon them.

Before we can be confirmed, we have to renew our baptismal promises. This is very important since Confirmation "completes" Baptism and allows for a further outpouring of the Holy Spirit upon us. In our Confirmation we receive a person, and the Holy Spirit

---

24 *Catechism of the Catholic Church,* # 683-686.

comes within us to teach us, convert us, and transform us so that we can know the Father and respond to the Lord's question: "Who do you say that I am?" and live a life according to the Spirit.[25]

The Faith of the Church

Guided by the Holy Spirit, we are led to an encounter with Jesus Christ and to make a personal decision for him. As we respond to his question, we realize that when we declare, "Jesus is Lord," we join a community of other believers who have also made this declaration. As we live our relationship with the Lord Jesus given to us at Baptism and Confirmation, so we enter into a relationship with all other believers. It is important that we realize that we are not alone in our faith. We are members of a community of faith.[26]

This leads us to a very important distinction. No one has an individual relationship with the Lord Jesus in the sense that individual means an esoteric, "me and Jesus" rapport. Rather, every human being is called to have a personal relationship with the Lord Jesus in the midst of the community of faith, within the people to whom God is united by a covenant. There is no "me and Jesus," but rather a "we and Jesus" in the life of faith. It is important that we understand the difference between "individual" and "personal." My faith truly depends on others, and the faith of others depends on my faith. We never walk alone

---

25   *Catechism of the Catholic Church*, # 1302-1305.
26   *Catechism of the Catholic Church*, # 758-760, 790-792, 1271.

as believers, but we are united to one another by Baptism and our personal decision for Jesus Christ.

"We Have Believed"

As St. Peter proclaimed that Jesus was the Christ, the Son of the living God, so he also made several other tremendous declarations in the public ministry of the Lord Jesus. On one occasion, the Lord spoke about the Eucharist and told his disciples:

> I am the living Bread which came down from heaven; if any one eats of this bread, he will live forever; and the bread which I shall give for the life of the world is my flesh. (Jn 6:51)

And the Lord continued:

> Truly, truly, I say to you, unless you eat the flesh of the Son of man and drink his blood, you have no life in you; he who eats my flesh and drinks my blood has eternal life, and I will raise him up at the last day. (Jn 6:53–54)

After this teaching, some of the Lord's disciples said, "this is a hard saying; who can listen to it?" and many of them "drew back and no longer walked with him." On this occasion, as the Lord's human nature was feeling great sorrow, he turned and asked the apostles, "Will you also go away?" In his answer to the Lord, St. Peter not only spoke from his own faith but from the faith of the community of apostles, as he told the Lord: "Lord, to whom shall we go? You have the words of eternal

life, and we have believed and have come to know, that
you are the Holy One of God" (Jn 6:68–69). St. Peter
spoke in the plural on behalf of the communal faith of
the Church. The chief apostle's personal faith was very
important, but it was part of a communal faith that was
beyond just one person. As each of us declares our faith,
we make our own the faith of the Church, the full Body
of Christ.

Summit and Source

It is very fitting that St. Peter would speak of the Church's
faith in the context of the Eucharist, of the Lord Jesus as
the living bread come down from heaven. The Eucharist
is properly understood as the summit and source of
the entire Christian life. Everything we do points to the
Eucharist, and from the Eucharist we find the strength to
do all other good things. In the Eucharist (a Greek word
meaning "thanksgiving") we celebrate as a community
that the Lord is present and among us.[27]

The Lord promised that he would not leave us
orphans (cf. Jn 14:18), and he is present to us in the com-
munity of faith, in his ordained shepherds, in the Sacred
Scriptures, and most especially in the Eucharist. In the
Eucharist, under the appearance of bread and wine, the
Lord Jesus makes his dwelling among us.[28]

Many years ago, when one of my nephews was just
a little guy, I took him to our local parish church and

---

27   Catechism of the Catholic Church, #1323-1327.
28   Catechism of the Catholic Church, #1374-1377, 1381.

showed him the different sacramentals, the statues, the Stations of the Cross, and then I showed him the tabernacle. As we approached the sanctuary, it was entertaining to see him try genuflect. But when I told him that Jesus lived in the tabernacle, he looked at me with disbelief, and said, "Uncle, it's too little," I laughed, but he was serious. So I explained that the tabernacle was like the one-man tent that his grandpa used for hunting. It was little, but someone could fit in it. That was enough for him. I was edified as I imagined that if I were to open the tabernacle, my nephew would expect to see Jesus lying down in a sleeping bag and waving to him. This is a good story because it illustrates a great and consoling truth: God has pitched his tent with us (cf. Jn 1:14).

The Eucharist is not "extra Catholic stuff" or "icing on the cake" of Christian discipleship, but it lies at the very core of our Christian identity. Our Baptism and Confirmation point us to the Eucharist, and as we seek to re-live the Paschal Mystery in our lives, we see in the Eucharist the sacramental re-presentation of that tremendous mystery—the passion, death, and resurrection of Jesus Christ—and from that celebration we receive renewed vigor and zeal, strength and inspiration as Christian believers.[29] In the Eucharist, the Lord is among us, and once again he turns to each of us and asks: "Who do you say that I am?"

---

29   Catechism of the Catholic Church, #1382-1383.

Cloud of Witnesses

As we near the time to make a personal decision for Jesus Christ, we realize in the light of the Eucharist, that we are a communion of holy ones. We comprehend in deeper ways that all the baptized are re-born into a vocation of holiness and are truly "saints." We can begin to see that there is a unity, a communion, among all the saints, all the holy ones in Jesus Christ. We can see that this communion is not just with a specific, local community, or even with all believers throughout the world today, but that this communion—directed to the Father, held in the very body of the risen Christ, and enlivened by the Holy Spirit—goes beyond this life, beyond even death.[30]

Whenever a believer dies in this life, he shares in the Resurrection of Jesus Christ, and joins what the Sacred Scriptures call the "cloud of witnesses" (cf. Heb 12:1). These witnesses who responded to the Lord's question with answers like those given by St. Paul, St. Thomas, and St. Peter and entered into a relationship with the Lord Jesus, surround us and offer us their help. These friends of God, our older brothers and sisters in the faith, are with us, and they spur us on to victory in Jesus Christ. They stand on the sidelines of our own discipleship, and they offer us their friendship, example, encouragement, and prayers. As we respond to the Lord's question and enter into a relationship with the Lord Jesus, we enter into a whole range of new friendships and realities beyond this world. We are able to worship God without fear, and are

---

30   *Catechism of the Catholic Church*, #954-959.

filled with a deep wonder at ourselves and the Church in Jesus Christ.[31]

Mother of the Church

Amidst this cloud of witnesses born from faith, none shines brighter or offers us more in Jesus Christ than the Blessed Virgin Mary, the mother of God and the first Christian disciple. As the Lord Jesus hung on the cross, dying of excruciating suffocation, he nevertheless said to St. John and to all Christians: "Behold, your mother!" (Jn 19:27).[32]

Always an advocate for believers, Mary perpetually points us to her divine Son. When praised by Elizabeth, she turned the praise to God and exclaimed: "My soul magnifies the Lord, and my spirit rejoices in God my savior" (Lk 1:46–47). At the wedding feast of Cana, she encouraged the Lord Jesus to work his first public miracle and to initiate his ministry. At Cana, she said to the servants, as she says to us now: "Do whatever he tells you" (Jn 2:5). At Pentecost, she was present as the Holy Spirit was sent upon the apostles and they began to preach the Gospel (Acts 1:14). She was and is always the mother of faith and of the Church.[33] Mary directs us to the Lord, and guides us to give a generous answer to his question: "Who do you say that I am?"

---

31 *Catechism of the Catholic Church*, #949-953.
32 *Catechism of the Catholic Church*, #964-970.
33 *Catechism of the Catholic Church*, #971-972.

Personal Decision for Jesus Christ

We are presented with the Lord's question. We have seen his great love for us, and we have heard the powerful testimony of St. Paul, St. Thomas, and St. Peter. Now, we have to discern and decide how we will answer. The invitation offered to us in Jesus Christ is not one that we merit or could have demanded. He invites us to decide for him because he first decided for us (Jn 15:16). The Lord Jesus freely gives the invitation in love. So, who is Jesus to us? How will we respond to his question?

Having the Lord's question before us, we join the great communion of saints as we respond to the Lord, and make our own the declaration of the holy ones: "Jesus Christ is Lord," "My Lord and my God," "You are the Christ, the Son of the living God." We say: "I follow you, Jesus, you are my Lord, Savior, Companion, Healer, Confidant, and Friend. You are my Everything."

PART TWO

"Why do you call me 'Lord, Lord,'
and not do what I tell you?"
Luke 6:46

"TEACH US"

CHAPTER FOUR

First Conversion of the Spiritual Life

"Depart from me, for I am a
sinful man, O Lord."
Luke 5:8

Following Jesus

We have taken the word "Lord" from Luke, Chapter 11, and focused on Jesus' question: "Who do you say that I am?" This is an important question, since our answer to it rekindles the gift of God that was given to us in Baptism and Confirmation, and it establishes our relationship with Jesus. Since we have responded to the question acknowledging Jesus as Lord, we now actively seek to live as his friends and disciples. This motivates us to want to grow in a life of prayer and virtue.

This leads us to the second part of our book that takes "Teach Us" from Luke, chapter 11, and will use the question of the Lord Jesus: "Why do you call me 'Lord, Lord,' and not do what I tell you?" (Lk 6:46).

Virtue and the Lord's Question

In the Gospel according to St. Luke, the evangelist collects the Lord's teachings in what has come to be called the "sermon on the plain." As the sermon comes to an end, the Lord Jesus notes how we can tell a tree by the fruit it bears, and so we can tell whether a person is good or evil based on the spiritual fruits he bears in his life (Lk 6:43–45). The Lord then asks the disciples, as he asks us today: "Why do you call me 'Lord, Lord,' and not do what I tell you?"

After the question, Jesus gives the illustration of the two foundations upon which a house can be built. The Lord says that a person who hears his teachings and tries to live by them is like someone who builds his house on rock. When the flood rises and the stream breaks against that house, it is not shaken because it is built on rock. But, the Lord also says that a person who does not live by his teaching builds his house on a foundation of sand, and when the stream waters break, they will destroy the house, and "the ruin of that house would be great" (Lk 6:49).

The Lord, therefore, calls us to build the house of our faith on rock. He directs us to his teachings and wants us to know what it means to live an abundant life in him. By declaring Jesus as Lord, we are called to build on rock and to surrender our lives to him and allow his grace to work within us and transform us more into the likeness of God. Will we listen to him? Do we realize how much we need the Lord? Why do we call him "Lord," and then not do what he tells us?

As we want to grow in our discipleship, in our

declaration that "Jesus is Lord," we need to give attention to virtues, which are good habits that cooperate with God's grace. In our lives, virtue is the visible, tangible expression of our discipleship and of our desire for holiness in Jesus Christ. Virtue is a daily witness to our relationship with Jesus Christ, and to our declaration that he is the Lord of our lives.

Many spiritual books do not address virtue, but jump directly to spiritual theology or to methods of prayer. While these aspects are important, the role of virtue needs to be explored since it is an essential part of following the Lord and ordering our lives according to his teachings. We cannot simply learn how to pray, we must also learn how to live our prayer and follow the Lord Jesus in both virtue and prayer.

An example might help us. Imagine if someone was to learn how to sail, and this would-be sailor studied all the specifics and skills of sailing, memorized the parts of the boat and the wind patterns in his area. He learned everything he could. But when it came time to actually sail, his boat was placed on the dry side of a dam, and there was no water. We would feel sorry for such a sailor who learned so much, but who does not have the water he needs to sail. In the same way, for spiritual theology and methods of prayer to work, we need the grace of virtue. Both virtue and prayer are needed. The two form an amazing exchange between themselves as they each support and inspire the other in our discipleship to the Lord. With this understanding, how can we grow into a deeper life of virtue? Where do we begin?

St. Peter's First Conversion

As we begin our search to understand virtue better, let's go to the very first encounter between Jesus and Simon Peter on the shores of Lake Gennesaret. The Lord was preaching, and the crowds became so vast that he asked Simon to use his boat, so that they could preach away from the land and everyone could hear him. After the Lord was done preaching, he told Simon, "Put out into the deep and let down your nets for a catch" (Lk 5:4). One can imagine some internal hesitation since Jesus was a carpenter, not a fisherman, and Simon and the other fishermen had been fishing all night and had not caught anything.

Simon, however, did as Jesus had instructed, and he caught so many fish that the nets were about to tear and he had to call for extra help from the other boat. After Simon saw what the Lord had done, he fell down at Jesus' knees, and said, "Depart from me, for I am a sinful man, O Lord" (Lk 5:8). This is one of the few recorded requests of the Lord that he did not fulfill. Instead, Jesus told Simon Peter, "Do not be afraid; henceforth you will be catching men" (Lk 5:10). Simon Peter and his brother left everything and followed him that day. Why did Simon Peter have this response? Why did he ask the Lord to depart from him? How can this encounter between Jesus and Simon Peter help us to understand our own relationship with Jesus?

The First Conversion and the Purgative Way

In this encounter, St. Peter experiences a deep conversion. Conversion is a "turning away" from something so that there can be a "turning toward" something greater. St. Peter realized that the Lord Jesus was greater than his fishing business, his own interests, or anything in this world.[34] In our spiritual tradition, we would say that St. Peter experienced the first conversion and the beginning of the purgative way. This term—the purgative way—is very important in our discipleship.

The purgative way is one of three traditional "ways" in which we progress in stages to greater intimacy with God. The Scriptures describe this as moving through "grace upon grace" (Jn 1:16).

The three stages of the spiritual life reflect the gradual workings of God. As with humanity and the Church in the course of salvation history, so with each of us now in the midst of the Church, God progressively reveals himself and allows his grace to transform us into his likeness. So, what did we see in St. Peter's first conversion? How are we to understand this conversion in our own lives?

The first conversion happens in our lives when God bestows a great awareness upon us—usually through a crisis, difficulty, or a general sense of being lost. This can happen quietly in the soul, as with a parent dealing with the struggles of family life, or very dramatically in extreme circumstances, as with a drug addict who nearly dies from an overdose. In the case of St. Peter, he felt

---

34   *Catechism of the Catholic Church*, #1427-1433.

completely overwhelmed and was in a crisis as he realized his own fishing efforts were in vain. He felt lost, but when approached by Christ, he experienced his first conversion and turned to the Lord. The first conversion is a gift to each of us, a type of "wake up" call from the Lord Jesus.

St. Peter asked the Lord to depart because he saw that he was a "sinful man" and realized his own unworthiness. The first conversion has the rich spiritual fruit of allowing us to see our complete unworthiness and our utter need for Jesus Christ and the workings of grace.

If we accept the first conversion, then our soul enters the purgative way, which is the way of the beginner in the spiritual life. During the purgative way of the spiritual life, we are called to abandon a life according to the flesh and walk more faithfully with the Lord. In this process, we hear and truly feel the depth of the Lord's question within our souls: "Why do you call me 'Lord, Lord,' and not do what I tell you?"

Different Phases of the Purgative Way

The purgative way is an interior hallowing of our souls and of our way of life. It is an ordering of our self to the person of Jesus Christ. In the purgative way, God's grace brings about a re-living of the Paschal Mystery—Christ's passion, death, and resurrection—within us in a profound way marked by purification, healing, and a reconstitution of who we are in Jesus Christ. As St. Paul writes: "Until we all attain to the unity of the faith and of the knowledge of the Son of God, to mature manhood, to the measure of the stature of the fullness of Christ. . . . We are to grow up in every way into him who is the head, into Christ" (Eph 4:13,15).

The purgative way has two principal phases within our souls: first, a time of consolation; and secondly, a time of darkness and desolation. These phases can be repeated within our souls depending on our faithfulness to the Lord Jesus. For example, if we backslide in our discipleship, then the purgative way could repeat itself.

After a first conversion, the beginning of the purgative way begins with great graces of consolation. We can imagine that during this initial phase, God throws a grand party in our soul. There are party guests, noisemakers, balloons, laughing, and a large cake with our face on it. Since the soul is just beginning the journey of the spiritual life, God comforts and indulges it to help us to persevere. Spiritual masters have diverse opinions, but the general consensus is that this period of consolation can last for up to three months depending on our personality and spiritual maturity.

After our soul has been immersed in consolation, the next phase of the purgative way is much harder and more properly purgative. We can imagine that grand party in our soul, and then all of a sudden the lights are turned out, the guests disappear, the noise is silenced, and our soul feels alone, restless in the dark. In this process the graces of consolation are replaced by the graces of obedience (which comes from a Latin word meaning "to listen"). Our soul is now called to persevere through a purification that allows it to worship the God of consolation, rather than the consolations of God. In this darkness of the purgative way, God orders our soul and leads it to spiritual maturity. While we may not feel it, God is, nevertheless, closer to us and is able to bring about a greater work within us than in the time of consolation. It is very important that we realize the normality and purpose of this darkness. Oftentimes, those who are taken from the time of consolation and who do not understand discipleship falsely believe that the time of darkness is an indication that they have done something wrong, or have offended God, or have been abandoned by him. None of these are true, and in the purgative way the knowledge of our discipleship and the workings of God is a tremendous help for us to mature in our emotions and grow in God's grace.

During the purgative way God heals our old wounds, lessens our egotism, grows our spirit, exposes our inordinate self-love, and names any bad spirits within us. He shows us the depravity of sin and its tragic consequences to our relationship with him, our world, and our neighbor. In the purgative way, we struggle and wrestle to abandon sin and our wayward attraction to sin. We begin to yearn for virtue, we want to fully live with Jesus as our Lord, and we desperately desire to live a life in the Spirit. The attraction of sin and the desire for holiness cause a tension within our souls. St. Paul summarizes this best:

> I do not understand my own actions. For I do not
> do what I want, but I do the very thing I hate. . . .
> For I do not do the good I want, but the evil I do not

want is what I do. Wretched man that I am! Who
will deliver me from this body of death? Thanks be
to God through Jesus Christ our Lord! (Rom 7:15,
19, 24–25)

Sound familiar? St. Paul himself struggled to do the
good he desired and avoid the evil he did not want to do.
In this intense exchange within himself, he almost sur-
renders to a sense of complete desolation, but then he
turns to Jesus and gives that powerful declaration: "Who
will deliver me... Thanks be to God through Jesus Christ
our Lord."

As we seek to be purged from all obvious and sensual
sins, let us turn again to St. Paul, who writes: "And those
who belong to Jesus Christ have crucified the flesh with
its passions and desires" (Gal 5:24). Also in the purgative
way, as we seek to be cleansed from the lusts of the world,
St. Paul continues: "But far be it from me to glory except
in the cross of our Lord Jesus Christ, by which the world
has been crucified to me, and I to the world" (Gal 6:14).

St. Paul describes this process as the "old person" giving way to the "new person" in Jesus Christ. He writes:

We know that our old self was crucified with him
so that the sinful body might be destroyed, and we
might no longer be enslaved to sin. (Rom 6:6)

And he observes:

For those who live according to the flesh set their
minds on the things of the flesh, but those who live
according to the Spirit set their minds on the things

of the Spirit . . . for if you live according to the flesh
you will die, but if by the spirit you put to death the
deeds of the body you will live. (Rom 8:5, 13)

In this experience and the teachings of St. Paul, we see
the depth and purpose of the purgative way: we see our
own sinfulness and helplessness, and we come to fully
know and believe how much we need the Lord Jesus. In
the purgative way, we find an interior summons to abandon a life of sin and self-centeredness and to seek a life of
love and self-donation.[35]

In the purgative way, God lets us fully experience
our own weakness and our total helplessness in trying to
falsely solve our own essential dilemma: "I am not where
I need to be, and I cannot get myself where I need to be."
This is the most basic and principal lesson of the purgative way: we cannot change without God. We must come
to completely and deeply believe this lesson if we are to
grow in our relationship with God.

There is a powerful story of a man who had a long-
standing and spiraling addiction to drugs. He overdosed
several times, and on one such occasion he was rushed to
the hospital and it was feared that he would die. The man
survived and afterwards he wanted to change his life.
This was his first conversion. He felt a great peace and
consolation with his desire to change. This was the initial
consolation of the purgative way. The man was sent to a
rehabilitation center, and for the first few days of recov-
ery, he was in intense detoxification. He describes that his

---

35   *Catechism of the Catholic Church*, #2012-2015.

body shook, jerked, and twisted uncontrollably. He could not even manage his own body, and he felt that he had lost everything. This was the darkness of the purgative way. The man said that the only words going through his mind were from St. Paul: "Work out your own salvation with fear and trembling, for God is at work in you . . ." (Phil 2:12–13). After he passed through his detoxification, he had a long road of healing and rebuilding his interior life, his passions, and his desires, but this man saw and understood the purgative way. He accepted it and let God work within him.

The Purpose of the Purgative Way

As God works in the soul during the purgative way, we should understand that God is present and bringing about a new identity within us. This is not easy, and the process can be a time of great anxiety and restlessness. The role of our emotions can be difficult in the purgative way, and they will need to be matured as our capacity for love increases. The purgative way is a time for vigilance and a time to actively pursue the basic attitude of a "new person" in Jesus Christ.

The purpose of the purgative way is to help us to live an ordered life in our relationship with God in Jesus Christ. It is how our Baptism and Confirmation are fully rekindled and how the Paschal Mystery becomes a reality in our lives, as we are incorporated and assimilated fully into Jesus Christ. The law of God, always a demanding tutor in the purgative way, is a preparation for us to be free and to allow virtue to grow within us and for us to live a life according to the Spirit. The purgative way helps grace to slowly enlighten our minds, strengthen our wills, mature our emotions and draw us ever closer to Jesus Christ, as he asks us: "Why do you call me 'Lord, Lord,' and not do what I tell you?" In the purgative way, we realize our brokenness and weakness—"Depart from me, for I am a sinner, O Lord," and "Wretched man that I am! Who will deliver me?"—and we come to know and feel deeply how much we truly need Jesus Christ, who alone can save us.

We hear the Lord's question, and we want to follow him. The purgative way is our first step to seeking the Lord Jesus, desiring to be his friends and disciples, and wanting generously to do all that he tells us.

CHAPTER FIVE

Virtue and Life in the Spirit

"He taught them."
Matthew 5:2

Being Taught by Jesus

The Lord Jesus asks us a penetrating question: "Why do you call me 'Lord, Lord,' and not do what I tell you?" It is a question that goes to the very heart of our discipleship. Will we obey our Lord's commands and align our wills with his? This inquiry leads us to explore a life of virtue, which is an opportunity to manifest both our relationship with the Lord Jesus and our desire to do what he asks of us. Nothing is more tangible than holiness, and virtue displays this tangibility in our daily lives. This pursuit of virtue is often not an easy one, and it will require a living out of the Paschal Mystery within us: a dying to ourselves, so that we can live for Christ. For this to happen well, we will need to confidently accept a purgative way within our lives in order to deepen and grow in our discipleship.

In the Lord's public ministry, he preached and illustrated many powerful and liberating truths. On one occasion when a large crowd was with him, the Lord went up a small mountain and began to teach the crowds. This has been collected by St. Matthew and is called the Sermon on the Mount. In this sermon, which spans three chapters (Mt 5–7), the Lord Jesus presented the fulfillment of the Old Testament and the advent of a New Testament. The Lord was attentive to his listeners and patiently explained to them, and to us today, this new way he has opened for us and how we are to live now as his friends and disciples. The Lord showed us what it means to follow him and allow his grace to transform us.

In our own discipleship, we need to turn to the Lord and regularly ask him to teach us these lessons again. As we desire to follow him, we should seek to recognize what a relationship with Jesus looks like, and what it means practically to live a life according to the Spirit.

Law and Virtue

As we ask the Lord to teach us, we have to understand the importance of God's law. When we speak of God's law, we do not mean the ceremonial law of the Old Testament. This law was fulfilled in the body of Jesus Christ (cf. Eph 2:14–16). This ceremonial law was dispensed by its fulfillment and now has no binding force on God's children in the new covenant. This is why we do not sacrifice animals, why we are not bound to follow dietary restrictions, and why the Sabbath could be moved from Saturday to Sunday, the day of Resurrection.

Beyond the ceremonial law, however, there is a moral law. This is God's law. Even as the Lord Jesus fulfilled the moral law, it is still binding on God's children since it helps to order our nature and prepare us for virtue and a life in the Spirit. Understanding this difference between the ceremonial and moral law, it is very important for us to understand the essential role of God's moral law in our discipleship and in our desire for virtue.

While we were created good, as children of Adam and Eve we each have a fallen nature and a disordered attraction to evil and waywardness. At times, we can create a law according to our own flesh—the flesh being an inordinate desire for evil, and not necessarily a synonym for our body—and we can allow ourselves to be ruled by a false law. We can rationalize and justify all kinds of evil and even call good things evil and evil things good. We need help. We need instruction. God's moral law, principally contained in the Ten Commandments, is our pedagogue, our tutor, which shows us the right way to live according to human nature and sound reason (cf. Gal 3:24–25).

The Ten Commandments

I. I am the Lord your God: you shall not have strange gods before me.

II. You shall not take the name of the Lord your God in vain.

III. Remember to keep holy the Lord's Day.

IV. Honor your father and mother.

V.   You shall not kill.

VI.   You shall not commit adultery.

VII.   You shall not steal.

VIII.   You shall not bear false witness
against your neighbor.

IX.   You shall not covet your neighbor's
wife.

X.   You shall not covet your neighbor's
goods. (Ex 20:2–17; Dt 5:6–21)

The moral law teaches us right from wrong, accuses us of our wicked actions, and denounces us in our waywardness. The moral law is a demanding tutor. It cannot heal or save us but is meant to instruct and educate us. Before we can begin to desire virtue, we have to first allow God's law to teach us. By showing us our sin, we are able to see the virtue that is offended and seek that virtue in our discipleship.[36] As we juggle the accusation of the law on one hand and our desire for virtue on the other, we see the importance of the purgative way in our discipleship, as it lessens our desire for sin and deepens our new attraction to virtue.

Freedom and Virtue

As we allow God's law to teach us, it prepares us for freedom. Freedom is often poorly defined as an ability to do

---

36   *Catechism of the Catholic Church,* #1950-1974.

whatever we want, but freedom is actually the ability to do what is right. If we are left to our own devices, we are not free. Freedom is an openness to God that allows the Holy Spirit to work within us. Freedom is a maturity of the soul that empowers us to act above our passions and desires, to see the proper order of things, and to do what is right. Freedom is our inheritance as Christian disciples. We have to grow into it and safeguard it so that our freedom itself does not become enslaved.[37] St. Paul summarizes these truths when he writes:

> For freedom Christ has set us free; stand fast therefore, and do not submit again to a yoke of slavery. (Gal 5:1)

And again, the apostle writes:

> Now the Lord is the Spirit, and where the Spirit of the Lord is, there is freedom. (2 Cor 3:17)

Via not Versus

This understanding of freedom from St. Paul is very helpful to us as we try to hear the Lord's question, "Why do you call me 'Lord, Lord,' and not do what I tell you?" We want to do whatever the Lord asks of us, but to live in this way, we must be free. We rely and depend on our freedom to live as friends and disciples of the Lord. Oftentimes, we want to draw a contradiction between God's law and freedom, seeing the two in tension, as one versus the other. The reality, however, is that there is no "versus"

---

37   *Catechism of the Catholic Church*, #1730-1742, 1763-1770.

between God's law and freedom, but rather a rapport of "via," meaning "by way of," which demonstrates that the law is in service to freedom and freedom benefits from the discipline of the law. The law helps us to be free. The law and freedom mutually need each other, and together they pave the way for virtue in our lives.

Virtue Born from Freedom

As we accept the instruction of God's law, and allow ourselves to experience true freedom in the Spirit, we begin to see the development and growth of virtue in our lives. Virtue is best understood as a good habit that governs our actions, orders our passions, and guides our conduct according to faith and reason.[38] As the law secures our freedom, so the law and freedom become the means for grace to ennoble us to exercise virtue in our discipleship.[39] This helps us to answer the Lord's question, "Why do you call me 'Lord, Lord,' and not do what I tell you?"

There was a young woman who was responsible for the care of her elderly mother. She felt bound to honor her mother. She took her to doctor's appointments, went grocery shopping for her, and sat and listened to her mother complain and repeat stories. Eventually, by fulfilling God's law of honoring her mother, the woman was able to experience a freedom of spirit, and this deepened and enlivened her relationship with her mother. The woman saw a more sincere gentleness and patience

---

38   *Catechism of the Catholic Church*, #1803-1804.
39   *Catechism of the Catholic Church*, #1810-1811.

within herself that she did not know she possessed. By the woman's obedience, virtue was born and she was able to enjoy a life in the Spirit.

Another example. The story is told of a young adult who could have lied and spread untruths in order to avoid and prevent some severe consequences. Accepting the instruction given by God's law, however, she would not lie and was accountable for her mistakes. Through this action and many others, she developed a strong sense of integrity and an aura of peace seemed to always surround her. She allowed herself to be disciplined by the law, which made her free, and this freedom gave birth to virtue in her.

Faith, Hope, and Charity

As we come to understand in a deeper and more expansive way how much God desires to work within us, and how our cooperation with grace is needed, we should be inspired by a tremendous desire to grow in virtue and allow God to make us holy, to help us to live as saints, and to do whatever he tells us.

The three principal virtues are called the theological virtues: faith, hope, and charity. They are called theological because they pertain directly to our participation in the life of God ("theos" is the Greek word for "God"). The theological virtues are infused virtues, and are different from their natural counterparts. For example, we might have faith in a teacher who tells us that a place called Australia exists, even though we have never been there. This is natural faith. Theological faith is when God shares his own knowledge of himself with us so that we can believe in him. This is an unmerited gift and one that immediately involves us in God's own life. The theological virtues are the foundation of all Christian moral activity, and the basis of all other virtues in our discipleship.[40] How should we understand them in our relationship with the Lord?

Faith is a share in God's own knowledge of himself. Our faith can move from belief in God's existence, to a belief in God based on trust, to the full expression of faith, which is believing "in God" within God himself. Our knowledge of God is not simply a collection of facts, but a true knowledge that is a participation in his own life. This level of faith calls for a total commitment from us, and is a share on our part in the Beatific Vision of heaven while we are still in this life.[41]

Hope is a share in God's eternity. Hope leads us to desire heaven as our happiness and to see this life in the light of eternity and its joys. Hope is a complete trust in God that relies on his promises and knows of his goodness. It inspires and purifies us. Hope orders our desires and expectations. It keeps us from discouragement and sustains us in times of abandonment and suffering. Hope gives us an eternal perspective, and it teaches us that life is not a problem to be solved, but a mystery to be lived.[42]

Charity is a share in God's own Trinitarian love. We love "in" God and seek to love our neighbors in his love.

---

40   *Catechism of the Catholic Church*, #1812-1813.
41   *Catechism of the Catholic Church*, #1814-1816.
42   *Catechism of the Catholic Church*, #1817-1821.

It heals us from egotism and an attraction to pleasure or power. Charity is seeking the authentic good of others in God, and is a willingness to even suffer and humble ourselves for the sake of another. Charity is the fulfillment of the Law and the prophets. It is the form of all other virtues and inspires all other virtues in the Christian way of life. St. John identifies God as love (1 Jn 4:8), and St. Paul says that faith and hope are fulfilled and that "only love endures" (1 Cor 13:13). The spiritual masters, all in different ways, assert that if we want to know what charity is, we only have to look at the cross. The Lord displays on Calvary the full definition of charity.[43]

The theological virtues are essential to the Christian way of life, and we are all summoned to live and exercise them in our discipleship. These virtues are so important that the entire program of Pope Emeritus Benedict XVI revolved around them. Benedict wrote three encyclicals, or teaching letters, entitled: *God Is Love, Saved in Hope,* and *Truth in Love.* He also co-wrote an encyclical with Pope Francis entitled *Light of Faith.*

The Cardinal Virtues

After the theological virtues follow four other virtues: prudence, justice, fortitude, and temperance. These virtues play a pivotal role in our discipleship, which is why they are referred to as the "cardinal virtues" (from the Latin word *cardo,* which means "hinge").[44] In learning

---

43   *Catechism of the Catholic Church,* #1822-1829.
44   *Catechism of the Catholic Church,* #1805.

about these virtues, we hear the Lord's question to us: "Why do you call me 'Lord, Lord,' and not do what I tell you?" These virtues flow from the theological virtues, and they form a dynamic reality with them. They can help us to hear the Lord in our lives and do all that he tells us.

The first cardinal virtue is prudence. It is hailed as the most important virtue after the theological virtues since it discerns the state of affairs in our lives and orders the response of all the other virtues to what is the greater good. Prudence guides our conscience and always seeks the good in situations.[45]

The second cardinal virtue is justice, which is giving God and our neighbor their just due. It promotes the common good, as well as respect and harmony among all people.[46]

The third cardinal virtue is fortitude. This virtue ensures firmness in difficulty and constancy in the pursuit of the good. It strengthens our resolve to resist temptations and helps us to overcome obstacles in our moral lives. Fortitude conquers fear and leads us to renounce and sacrifice things for a just cause.[47]

The fourth cardinal virtue is temperance, which moderates our attraction to pleasure and provides a balance to us in our use of created goods. Temperance assures our will's mastery over our instincts and keeps

---

45   *Catechism of the Catholic Church*, #1806.
46   *Catechism of the Catholic Church*, #1807.
47   *Catechism of the Catholic Church*, #1808.

our desires within the limits of goodness.[48]

All other virtues, such as compassion, obedience, humility, etc., flow from the theological and cardinal virtues. The exercise of virtue shows us that we are truly the sons and daughters of God as we imitate his life and open ourselves to be transformed into his likeness by grace.

Virtue and Holiness

Virtue is the Lord's daily call that tells us what to do in our lives. And there is nothing more tangible and practical in this world than holiness. It is more real than the physical objects in front of us. And virtue shows us holiness. It helps us to see, hear, taste, smell, and touch holiness. Virtue shows us what a relationship with God looks like in this world.

Virtue and the Spirit

In our discipleship, as we develop habits and exercise virtues, we grow in our relationship with the Lord Jesus. In our lives, we look for opportunities to do whatever he tells us, and we seek to be like him in all our ways.

As virtue flourishes, the Holy Spirit is able to bestow particular graces and a certain formation upon our souls. What in the past appeared to be lofty spiritual states suddenly become very lived realities in our lives. The Beatitudes become our way of life.[49]

---

48   *Catechism of the Catholic Church*, #1809.
49   *Catechism of the Catholic Church*, #1716-1724,

Beatitudes

- Blessed are the poor in spirit, for theirs is the kingdom of heaven.

- Blessed are those who mourn, for they shall be comforted.

- Blessed are the meek, for they shall inherit the earth.

- Blessed are those who hunger and thirst for righteousness, for they shall be satisfied.

- Blessed are the merciful, for they shall obtain mercy.

- Blessed are the pure in heart, for they shall see God.

- Blessed are the peacemakers, for they shall be called sons of God.

- Blessed are those persecuted for righteousness' sake, for theirs is the kingdom of heaven.

- Blessed are you when men revile you and persecute you and utter all kinds of evil against you falsely on my account. Rejoice and be glad, for your reward is great in heaven, for so men persecuted the prophets who were before you. (Mt 5:3–12)

As we see the Beatitudes lived within us, we also see the fruits of the Holy Spirit, which are the "first fruits of eternal glory" manifested in our daily lives. The fruits of the Spirit, summarized by the Prophet Isaiah and St. Paul, are: charity, joy, peace, patience, kindness, goodness, generosity, gentleness, faithfulness, modesty, self-control, and chastity.[30]

The Beatitudes and the fruits of the Spirit reflect the full flourishing of virtue within us, and are the crown of God's work in our lives. This is the life in the spirit first bestowed on us at Baptism and Confirmation, and rekindled in us by our friendship and discipleship to the Lord Jesus.

As we hear the Lord's question, "Why do you call me 'Lord, Lord,' and not do what I tell you?" we can now say, "We call you 'Lord,' and we will do all that you tell us. Lead us, Lord, and we will follow."

---

50   *Catechism of the Catholic Church*, #1832.

CHAPTER SIX

Rule of Life

"Sanctify them in Truth."
John 17:17

Jesus Prays for Us

It is a great truth—Jesus intercedes for us—and it is a truth that should greatly inspire us. Every evening during his public ministry, the Lord would seclude himself from the apostles, and spend time in prayer to the Father. We do not know the content of that prayer in general, but we were given a glimpse of it in the Lord's High Priestly Prayer contained in the Gospel according to St. John, Chapter 17. In this prayer, right before his arrest and the beginning of his passion, the Lord speaks to the Father about us. He prays and intercedes for us. He asks the Father to sanctify us in truth. Why would Jesus intercede for us? What does this mean? What difference should this make in our lives?

The Lord presses us with his question: "Why do you call me 'Lord, Lord,' and not do what I tell you?" We see the Lord's love for us as he makes this petition of the Father. We should understand his request within the realm of our friendship and discipleship to the Lord

Jesus. As we follow the Lord and live out the Paschal Mystery, the Father is able to sanctify us in truth by the power of the Holy Spirit. But we have to cooperate and let God's grace work. How can we nurture this cooperation in our lives? What can help us remain open to the workings of God within us?

Our Christian Vocation

It is a powerful assertion in our world to announce that we are Christian. It is a strong vocation and counter-cultural way of life. Once, while describing the various titles given to the papacy, Pope St. John Paul II noted that of all the titles that the pope has received throughout history, none of them are as essential or foundational as the title "Christian." This is the most important identity we have, and even the pope, as the shepherd of the universal Church, most treasures his discipleship and sees his identity as a Christian as his most important identity, above all others.

Realizing and cherishing this vocation and identity is the beginning of our cooperation with God's work. From this deep gratitude, we understand that as Christians we are called to live differently than the unbeliever. We are summoned to a particular way of life. In fact, before we were called Christians, we were simply called members of "the Way." The title "Christian" came later, but emphasizes even more how we are called to follow the Lord Jesus "on the way" in the course of our daily lives (cf. Acts 9:2, 11:26).

We have already seen how the Lord Jesus had an

order, a schedule, of his time with the Father, and in the Acts of the Apostles we know that the early Christian community observed the set prayer times of the Temple, and would meet for the Eucharist, to pray together, study the writings of the Apostles, offer alms, and have holy fellowship (cf. Acts 2:43–47). In diverse ways, a recognized rule of life was understood and lived. It was a way for God's presence to be acknowledged, for the Christian person or the community to discern his will, and for the worship of God. This practice continues in the life of the Church, and should inspire us to ask: How do we acknowledge God's presence and follow him in our daily lives? What means is given to us that can help us to walk with the Lord throughout our day?

Rule of Life

The spiritual tradition of the Church passes along a means of holiness called a "Rule of Life." The rule of life is composed by each of us for our daily lives. It consists of different resolutions and commitments that span the diverse aspects of our discipleship, and is an active way for us to regularly acknowledge the Lord and seek to do all that he tells us. The rule of life is not a self-help tool, but a legitimate spiritual means by which we seek grace through both virtue and prayer so that we can draw ever closer to the Lord Jesus in our lives.

The rule of life is not merely a collection of rules that we juggle throughout the day, but a sincere recognition that the Lord has "rule" of our lives, and that we desire, more than anything throughout the day, to be in his presence and have a relationship with him.[51]

In composing a rule of life, we should always involve a spiritual director who can review our rule, and offer counsel on the different parts of it. The counsel of a spiritual director should always be followed, and rarely dismissed.[52]

How do we begin to compose a rule of life? What is our first step?

Two Foundational Principles

In wanting to compose a rule of life, we have to begin with two basic principles, which are the foundation and inspiration of a vibrant rule of life:

1) In our daily lives, have to always recognize the presence of God. In what is oftentimes called "the sacrament of the present moment," we should look for God in our daily tasks.[53] Rather than looking upon work as a burden, we can understand that Christ is there waiting to encounter us, and see our work as a source of solidarity with God and our neighbor. Rather than looking upon the duties of family life as a chore or source of frustration, we can look and see Christ in crying or complaining children, in the routine chaos of a home, and even in our tiredness of spirit. We are called to see the Lord present in all our joys and sorrows, triumphs and sufferings. This basic principle is essential for a good rule of life. A spiritual classic that helps us with this principle is

---

51　*Catechism of the Catholic Church*, #1434-1435.

52　*Catechism of the Catholic Church*, #2690.

53　Cf. *Catechism of the Catholic Church*, #2659.

Practicing the Presence of God by Brother Lawrence of the Resurrection.

2) Oftentimes, we want excitement, drama, and something new. The adrenaline is inspiring and the ambition is enchanting. But, if we are always looking for these types of twists and turns, then we will not be able to sustain a rule of life or grow substantially in the spiritual life. We have to calm things down and "sanctify our ordinary lives." In our relationship with the Lord Jesus, we have to be comfortable and satisfied with ordinary, even mundane, things in our lives. We have to let these become opportunities to see and encounter God.[54] These quiet exchanges are often the source of tremendous spiritual growth and insight. This principle is needed for a strong rule of life. A spiritual classic that can help us to fully live this principle is *Abandonment to Divine Providence* by Fr. Jean Pierre de Caussade.[55]

General Counsel

After these two foundational principles, there is some other general counsel that might be helpful as we compose our rule of life:

- It is very important that the rule of life is an act of discipleship. We want to be with the Lord, hear him, and do what he tells us in our daily lives, and the rule of life is a means

---

54   Cf. *Catechism of the Catholic Church*, #2660.
55   Fr. Jean Pierre de Caussade, *Abandonment to Divine Providence*, Charlotte, NC: TAN Books, 2010.

to deepening this relationship. The rule of
life is not merely a tool for self-improve-
ment or a competition with ourselves. No
medals or gold stars are given out after a
good rule of life!

- Our resolutions and commitments in the
  rule of life have to be eminently practical
  and realistic. If we have not been praying
  regularly, we cannot suddenly make a resolution to pray a holy hour or three rosaries
  every day. Also, if we have a strong habitual
  sin, we cannot simply say that we will not
  commit that sin anymore. These unrealis-
  tic resolutions would be like someone who
  says they are going to run a marathon, but
  have not even regularly run a single mile.
  In the rule of life, the goal is to start small
  and to stay practically minded. Initially, our
  purpose is simply to develop regular good
  habits, and then to deepen or expand what
  we have been doing.

- In sports, a team has to choose whether
  they will follow a person-to-person or a
  zone defense. In the same way, the rule of
  life has to be strategic. As we start a rule of
  life, we have to let the plan follow our daily
  lives, and then slowly allow it to mold and
  shape them. If our lives are very fluid, then

it would not be helpful to set resolutions at specific times, i.e.: "I'll pray the Divine Mercy Chaplet at 3:00 PM." It might be better to allow a zone approach and resolve to pray the Chaplet "in the afternoon." Again, the rule of life needs to be strategic so that it will help us to encounter the Lord throughout our day.

- In a rule of life there is always a delicate balance between flexibility and firmness. It is helpful for us to recognize where we usually fall on this spectrum, ie, "I'm usually very flexible with things," or, "I tend to be a stickler when it comes to commitments," etc. Having this knowledge of ourselves will help us approach our rule of life with good judgment, especially when a resolution needs to be held steadfastly, or adjusted, or even suspended. It is important to note that the whole purpose of having a rule of life is so that our day is ordered by our relationship with God. We cannot fall into either laxity or scrupulosity. On occasions when we have to evaluate our rule of life, a simple question can help: In this situation, what will help me and those around me to be closer to God?

- A rule of life might have several adjust-
  ments at first. These should be noted,
  and the rule of life should eventually be
  amended. It is a good and sound practice to
  regularly review and assess our rule of life.
  Again, a spiritual director can be a tremendous resource in this effort.

The Rule of Life: Two Parts

Having reviewed the foundational principles and some
general counsel, it is time for us to dive right into the
mechanics of the rule of life. How do we compose a rule
of life? What are the parts and details of a rule? How do
we get started?

The rule of life needs a strong motto. We have to
choose something from the Sacred Scriptures, such as
"Your kingdom come," "Remember me when you come
in your kingly power," "This is my beloved Son," "My Lord
and my God," or from the life of the Church: "For the
sake of his sorrowful passion," "Vivo Cristo Rey," "O God
of love, give me love." The motto is very important since
it will help us to persevere in our rule of life when we are
distracted, weak, or rebellious. The motto serves to call
us back to our rule of life and inspire us to faithfulness.

Rule of Life

Motto: ....

....

....

The rule of life consists of two parts: the Reform of Life (Particular Exam–) and our Spiritual Exercises.

Part One: Reform of Life (Particular Exam–)

The first part of the rule of life is called the Reform of Life, or the Particular Exam. This part focuses on opposing vice and developing a life of virtue. There are four major components of the Reform of Life.

- First, after prayer to the Holy Spirit, we must identify our dominant defect. This is the one bad spirit that most motivates our sin. It is usually one of the seven deadly sins: pride, envy, wrath, sloth, avarice, gluttony, or lust. While we are all guilty of all seven, it is important that we find the dominant vice in our lives. We should be very attentive in finding our dominant defect since sometimes what we think is our dominant defect is not actually the dominant defect. For example, someone is committing acts

of impurity. The dominant defect could
be lust, but it could also be wrath or pride.
Someone is a horrible gossip. The dominant
defect could be envy or avarice or pride.
Serious discernment is needed in identifying our dominant defect.[56]

- After we recognize our dominant defect,
  we will need to discern its opposing virtue.
  For example, if a person's dominant defect is
  wrath, the opposing virtue could be mercy,
  humility, gentleness, or another virtue. We
  have to deeply discern and identify what
  virtue would heal, mature, and conquer our
  dominant defect. This virtue is the focus of
  the Reform of Life (Particular Exam–), and
  the principal reason for this part of our rule
  of life. The focus needs to always stay on the
  desired virtue.[57]

- In identifying the opposing virtue, we now
  have to enter more deeply into our lives and
  try to find the specific areas of darkness that
  need conversion. We need to identify concrete manifestations of our dominant

---

56 The book, *Seven Capital Sins* by the Benedictine Sisters of
    Perpetual Adoration, could be a tremendous resource for
    this part of the Reform of Life. TAN Books.

57 A great book that combines an explanation of virtue with
    the lives of the saints is *A Year with the Saints: A Virtue for
    Every Month of the Year*. TAN Books.

defect. We can choose as many as we like, but oftentimes three is a good number since they can be easily remembered. The three manifestations should be as tangible and specific as possible. The healing and conquest of the dominant defect relies on this precision. For example, if we write that our dominant defect is pride and one manifestation is that we think we are better than other people, this is not helpful and will not bear great spiritual fruit. If we instead write that our dominant defect is pride and one manifestation is that we always make ourselves the center of attention in conversations, this is a good manifestation and there can be reform. The manifestations should be concrete, particular acts.[58]

- Once we name the manifestations of our dominant defects, we now have to make counter resolutions to heal and fight the manifestations. So, if our dominant defect is pride, and we make ourselves the center of attention in conversations, then our resolution will be to ask questions of other people in discussions and listen to what they say. The resolution should be as particular as

---

58   The spiritual classic, *Sin and its Consequences* (TAN Books) by Cardinal Manning, could be of tremendous help in recognizing the manifestations of sin in our lives.

the manifestation. It should immediately
address the manifestation and work to
expose and conquer it. As our desired virtue is our focus, so are our resolutions the
focus of the Reform of Life. This is where
the struggle for virtue becomes real. This is
where we allow grace to become resolutely
tangible in our lives. There should also be
a self-penance attached to the resolution in
case it is not done or done poorly. So, if we
are in a conversation, and we do not follow
our resolution, then a self-penance could be
that we do not watch television that evening, or we remove something enjoyable
from our lives. The role of self-penances is
essential to spiritual maturity and growth in
virtue.

In understanding the different components of the
Reform of Life (Particular Exam), it might be helpful to
see it outlined:

Reform of Life
(Particular Examen)

Dominant Defect: ....
....
....

Opposing Virtue: ....
....
....

Manifestations:

1) ....
   ....

2) ....
   ....

3) ....
   ....

Resolutions:

1) ....

....

SELF-PENANCE: ....

....

2) ....

....

SELF-PENANCE: ....

....

3) ....

....

SELF-PENANCE: ....

....

Part Two: Spiritual Exercises

After understanding the first part of the Rule of Life, it is important that we address the second part. Entitled, "Spiritual Exercises," this should not be confused with the proper *Spiritual Exercises* of St. Ignatius of Loyola. Those are a collection of meditations, whereas this part of the rule of life pertains to all the exercises of our spiritual soul to which we commit ourselves. As we do physical exercises to strengthen our bodies, so we need spiritual exercises to strengthen our soul. As an athlete has a regimen of certain exercises in a workout and certain exercises on specific days, so we must have a similar plan for our spiritual exercises.

The Spiritual Exercises are divided into four components: daily, weekly, monthly, and seasonally. In each component, we should list what we resolve and are committed to do. It is very important that we are realistic in our resolutions, and that we commit ourselves only to what we can practically complete at this point in our lives and in our discipleship. This is not the place for wishful thinking, but for practical, achievable commitments in order to grow in our relationship with the Lord Jesus.

In the daily component, some things to consider:

- Morning Prayers. Praying the Morning Offering and other prayers to begin our day, perhaps the Acts of Faith, Hope, and Charity. A manual of prayers can be of great help, and one option is *Catholic Prayers* by Thomas Nelson.[59]

- Liturgy of the Hours. This is the formal prayer of the Church. It consists of praying the Psalms, and is offered seven times a day.

- Meditation. Spending some time with the Lord in conversation. Speaking to him

---

59   Thomas A. Nelson, *Catholic Prayers*, Charlotte, NC: TAN Books, 2009.

from our hearts, and sharing with him our thoughts and state of affairs. As our meditation deepens, the use of specific prayer forms can helpful in developing our conversation with the Lord Jesus. The length of our meditation will be determined by our state in life and our spiritual habits. At times, spiritual guidebooks can be helpful. Two books that are incredible resources are the *Spiritual Exercises* of St. Ignatius of Loyola and the *Imitation of Christ* by Thomas à Kempis.[60]

- Daily Mass. If it is possible, the ability to attend daily Mass could be a great spiritual benefit for each of us and for our discipleship.

- Angelus. This prayer (or the Regina Caeli prayer in the Easter season) could be prayed three times a day. It is a prayer that honors the Incarnation and reminds us of God's presence among us.

- Sacred Scriptures. The devout reading of the Bible is of tremendous spiritual benefit to each of us. If possible, we should try to read from the Scriptures every day.

---

60   Thomas A. Kempis, *The Imitation of Christ*, Charlotte, NC: TAN Books, 2010.

- Spiritual Reading. If possible, some time every day (or a few days during the week) should be set aside for spiritual reading. This could be a necessary formation for us on aspects of our faith. Our reading could include books on spirituality, such as *The Introduction to the Devout Life* by St. Francis de Sales or *The Spiritual Life* by Fr. Adolphe Tanquerey, or a life of a saint, such as *The Life of Saint Francis* or *The Story of a Soul: The Life of St. Therese of Lisieux.*[61]

- Marian Devotion. The Rosary, a part of the Rosary, or some Marian devotion should be a part of our spiritual exercises.

- Examen. Offering a general or particular examen in the afternoon and/or in the evening can help us to daily discern the Lord's presence and his will in our lives.

- Evening Prayers. As the day comes to a close, the offering of prayers is the best way to conclude our activities and give our day to the Lord. Again, a manual of prayers can be helpful with this resolution.

---

61 St. Therese of Lisieux, *The Story of a Soul*, Charlotte, NC: TAN Books, 2010.

In the weekly component, some things to consider:

- Sunday Mass. This is truly the summit and source of our entire week. This is absolutely a non-negotiable. All the other commitments and resolutions of our rule of life depend on the Mass, especially on the Lord's Day.

- Holy Hour. Perhaps a weekly holy hour could be prayed on a specific day or at a specific time. If possible, Thursday is a favored day in honor of Holy Thursday and the Institution of the Eucharist.

- Friday Penance. As Christians, we are called to do some form of penance on every Friday of the year in honor of the Lord's passion and death. During the Fridays of Lent we are obliged to a meat abstinence. Outside of Lent, we are able choose our own penance. Our Friday penance is an obligation, and we should give particular attention to this act of devotion.

- Saturday Devotion. On Saturdays, we should look for a way to honor or show devotion to Our Lady. Since Saturday is devoted to Mary, some sign of affection to her is most appropriate.

- Bible Studies/Prayer Groups: As we live in

a community of faith, it is a good custom to participate in some form of Bible study or prayer group on a weekly basis. This type of study or fellowship can be extremely helpful to our discipleship.

In the monthly component, some things to consider:

- Confession. It is a spiritually healthy practice to go to confession regularly, certainly on a monthly basis (if not more).

- Spiritual Direction. It is a noble exercise to see a spiritual director at least every month. During this time, it is good to review and adjust the rule of life as needed.

- Devotions. It is a good practice to observe devotions during a certain month. Perhaps praying the Rosary daily during the month of October, or praying for the holy souls in Purgatory during November, etc. These devotions help us to live specific aspects of our discipleship and to grow in greater affinity for the different parts of our faith.

- Day of Recollection/Alms-giving: It is a strong practice to choose a day or a half-day every month to spend time in solitude and prayer, as well as in some form of charitable service and alms-giving. This will have to be lived according to our state in life, but should be present in some form in our spiritual exercises. A great resource that addresses both these aspects of our discipleship is the spiritual classic *Soul of the Apostolate* by Fr. Jean-Baptiste Chautard.[62]

In our seasonal component, some things to consider:

- Advent. Be sure to use the weeks of Advent for spiritual renewal. It is a noble practice to take on some additional spiritual exercise during Advent, i.e., a daily Rosary, deeper examens, broader alms-giving, etc. It is also praiseworthy to observe the "O Antiphons," or some other Advent devotional.

- Christmastide. The season of Christmas is an occasion to celebrate God's presence among us. It is an opportunity to fill our rule of life with deeper hope and joy.

- Lent. The season of Lent is the time of grand conversion in our faith. The Lenten weeks should be seen as a time to deepen and renew our entire rule of life, as well as a time to note and work on areas that are weak or have been neglected by us. It is a time to reflect on the Lord's passion, especially through the Stations of the Cross and

---

62   Fr. Jean-Baptiste Chautard, *The Soul of the Apostolate*, Charlotte, NC: TAN Books, 2009.

a pious reading of his sufferings. Lent is an annual, miniature catechumenate that helps us to prepare for the celebration of our Lord's Resurrection, and the renewal of our baptismal promises. We should be sure to use this season very prudently.

- Easter. The Easter season is the greatest celebration in the Church's year. It is a time to take the parts of our rule of life deeper (rather than adding things to them). The Easter season is the occasion to renew all things and re-focus them on the hope and joy of the Resurrection.

- Novenas. It is a helpful practice to observe Novena prayers periodically, perhaps for the feast day of a favored saint or a revered event in the life of our Lord or Our Lady. The book, *Thirty Favorite Novenas,* can be a good resource for us in this practice.[63]

- Marian Consecration. It is a most praise-worthy practice for us to prepare and offer a consecration to Our Lord through Our Lady, especially during the months of October and May (which have designations in honor of Mary). Such a consecration can help us to interiorize our Baptism and live more faithfully as friends and disciples of

---

63   *Thirty Favorite Novenas,* Charlotte, NC: TAN Books, 2009.

the Lord. There are different Marian con-
secrations, but the most cherished is that
of St. Louis de Montfort whose book, *True
Devotion to Mary*, explains the consecration
well and is a great help in understanding
this devotion.[64]

Having explained the different components of the
spiritual exercises, it might help us to see them in an
outline:

Spiritual Exercises

Daily: ....

....

....

....

....

....

....

....

....

....

---

64   St. Louis de Montfort, *True Devotion to Mary*, Charlotte, NC: TAN Books, 2010.

Weekly: ....

....

....

....

....

....

....

....

....

Monthly: ....

....

....

....

....

....

....

....

....

Seasonally: ....

....

....

....

....

....

....

....

....

....

Living Our Rule of Life

Now, it might happen that we see all of the options above and are a little overwhelmed. We should not be over-whelmed, since we will walk through our rule of life and slowly deepen or take on additional aspects that will help us to grow. For now, there are no expectations except that we realistically and practically discern what we are able to do, and that we do our best. As we move forward, we will adjust the rule of life so that it continues to be a resource for us to know of God's presence, grow in our relationship with him, and open ourselves so that he can "sanctify us in truth."

The Lord asks us, "Why do you call me 'Lord, Lord,' and not do what I tell you?" and in our rule of life, we say to him: "Lord, we love you. You are Lord, and we will do what you tell us. Come, and teach us."

PART THREE:

"What do you want me to do for you?"
Luke 18:41

"TO PRAY"

CHAPTER SEVEN

The Lord Among Us

"Their eyes were opened and they recognized Jesus."
Luke 24:31

The Lord's Question

The Lord desires to give us so much! So far, we have explored our relationship with Jesus and have come to recognize him as "Lord," then we were moved to have the Lord "Teach Us" as we desire a life of virtue, and now we turn to him and ask him to show us how "To Pray." In Part Three of our book, we will now pursue an explanation of prayer and specific aspects of our spiritual lives.

We turn to the Lord. As he was passing Jericho during his public ministry, a blind man was begging and heard a multitude of people going by. He asked what was going on and was told that Jesus of Nazareth was passing by. He cried out, "Son of David, have mercy on me!" People in the crowd told him to quiet down, but he cried out even louder. Jesus stopped and commanded him to be brought to him, and when the man came near to him, Jesus asked him, "What do you want me to do for you?"

This is the same question the Lord asks of us. The blind man said to Jesus, "Lord, let me receive my sight," and Jesus said to him, "Receive your sight; your faith has made you well" (Lk 18:42). This question of the Lord is the basis of Part Three of our book: "What do you want me to do for you?" What is our answer?

The Walk to Emmaus

We should immediately turn to the walk to Emmaus after Jesus' Resurrection. This story highlights many aspects of our endeavor to understand prayer and our relationship with the Lord Jesus.

The story is familiar to many of us. After Jesus' passion and death, two disciples left Jerusalem and were on their way to Emmaus, a journey of about seven miles. As they were walking, they talked about all the things that happened, and while they were discussing these matters, Jesus himself drew near and walked with them. He asked the disciples, "What is this conversation which you are holding with each other as you walk?" (Lk 24:17).

The disciples stood still, looked sad, and said to Jesus, "Are you the only visitor who does not know the things that have happened there in these days?" Jesus asked, "What things?" and the disciples recounted the events of the passion and death. The disciples expressed dismay because they had hoped that Jesus would redeem Israel. Jesus then opened the Scriptures to them, and from Moses to the prophets, he showed them how the Christ was to suffer these things in order to enter his glory (Lk 24:25–27).

As the conversation moved along, they drew near to the village where they were going, and Jesus appeared to be going farther, but they asked him to stay. So Jesus stayed with them, took bread and blessed and broke it, and gave it to them. Their eyes were opened and they recognized Jesus (Lk 24:31). At that, he vanished from their sight, and the disciples said to each other, "Did not our hears burn within us while he talked with us on the road, while he opened to us the Scriptures?" And they rose and returned that hour to Jerusalem and recounted what happened on the road and how Jesus was made known to them in the breaking of the bread (Lk 24:35).

Principal Points

From this amazing story, we can draw five principal points that will assist us in approaching a life of prayer:

- Jesus draws near to us on the way.
- Jesus explains to us the path to holiness.
- Jesus shows us the importance of the Sacred Scriptures.
- The Lord shows us his presence in the Eucharist.
- Jesus teaches us about community and evangelization.

Jesus Draws Near to Us

In the hustle and bustle of our lives, it is a great consolation that the Lord Jesus takes the initiative and approaches us. The providence of God, his fatherly care for us, is a humbling mystery that allows us to know of his presence in our lives. The Lord shows us this providence and comes directly to us "on the road" of our lives, of our suffering, confusion, anxiety, and of our joys, accomplishments, and hopes. The Lord is with us. Just as he asked the disciples about the events in Jerusalem, the Lord asks us: "What is happening in your lives?" He walks with us, listens to us, cares for us, and desires to be with us along the road of our lives.

The Path to Holiness

On the road of our lives, as the Lord approaches us, he seeks to show us the path to holiness. The Christ did not accomplish his mission in worldly glory or military victory as many wanted, but through humility and suffering. He explained this to the disciples on the road to Emmaus, as he also wants to teach us. The Lord seeks to instruct us about suffering. If we wish to manifest his heavenly glory, and if we want to be in a relationship with him then we have to be willing to suffer and to understand the workings of grace even in the midst of difficulty and hardship.

As the Lord taught the disciples, their hearts burned within them. This is an example of what our spiritual tradition calls the illuminative way.

Illuminative Way

In the spiritual life, after we have passed through the purgative way, we enter into the illuminative way, the way of enlightenment. One of the essential marks of this enlightenment is that we do not perceive God outside of us, but rather within us. Like the disciples on the way to Emmaus, our hearts burn within us. In the illuminative way, there is a new level of peace and tranquility in our soul, which is a welcome reprieve after the purgative way. This does not mean that there is no longer any purification needed within us. God is still working. The spiritual masters present the illuminative way as a period of calm after the storm of the purgative way; however, just as after a physical storm there is debris that needs to be picked up and cleared away, so in the spiritual life the illuminative way is clearing debris in our soul. The work of the illuminative way is less dramatic, and tends to happen more deeply within our interior lives and is related to a refined conversion of heart to the Lord Jesus. In this way of the spiritual life, our prayer slows down and less activity is needed in our relationship with God. We desire to be at rest in God and he speaks more to us in the solitude of our hearts.

The Sacred Scriptures

As the Lord met the disciples on the way to Emmaus, he began to teach them, and in his instruction he drew their attention to the Scriptures. This demonstrates a powerful truth, expressed by St. Paul to St. Timothy:

> All Scripture is inspired by God and profitable for teaching, for reproof, for correction, and for training in righteousness, that the man of God may be

complete, equipped for every good work. (2 Tim
3:16–17)

As Christians, we need to see the utter importance
of the Sacred Scriptures in our discipleship. We need to
read and study the Bible, memorize its passages, and seek
to understand its truths. The Bible is God's love letter
to humanity. It is a syllabus for us on the purpose and
meaning of life, and a disclosure of the essential truths
of human life given by God. Many people approach God
as a stranger, and so his ways seem strange. Through the
Scriptures, Jesus showed the disciples the truth about
his passion and death. In reading the Sacred Scriptures,
we too can come to know God better, and to see how he
works in our lives and in our world. But the Bible can be
intimidating. Where should we start? How can we read
the Bible well and receive all that God wants to give us?

Reading the Bible

The Bible can be confusing at first. Many people do not
realize that the word Bible means "library" and, as a
library, it contains many different kinds of books, such
as history books, stories, wisdom literature, rituals, pro-
phetic writings, and letters. We have to understand the
proper genre of each book, and we need to know that
the Bible was not written chronologically. So, many people will start reading Genesis and then move to Exodus
(which are both narrative books), and then suddenly
hit Leviticus and not know what is going on. Leviticus
is a ritual book, literally a handbook for Old Testament

priests on how to offer the sacrifices. So, how can we begin?

Here are a few suggestions:

- If we want to try and read the Bible in a chronological narrative, then we will want to read what are called the narrative books. These are: Genesis, Exodus, Numbers, Joshua, Judges, 1 and 2 Samuel, 1 and 2 Kings, Ezra, Nehemiah, 1 Maccabees, Luke, and Acts of the Apostles.

- It might be helpful for us to read a summary of the Bible and its different parts. A great resource is *Introduction to the Bible* by Fr. John Laux.[65]

- There are thirty-one days in a full month, and there are thirty-one proverbs in the Book of Proverbs in the Old Testament. An easy way for us to introduce the Scriptures into our daily lives would be for us to read the proverb that matches the day of the month, (i.e., on January 6, we will read Proverb 6, etc.).

- The Gospel according to St. Mark is the shortest of the four gospels. Sometimes

65   Fr. John Laux, *Introduction to the Bible*, Charlotte, NC: TAN Books, 2009.

called "the handbook of Christianity,"
it is only sixteen chapters and is a very
quick read. We could choose to read a
chapter or a part of a chapter every day.

These are some options, but however we do it, the
most important thing is that we are reading God's living
word and allowing it to be a part of our discipleship and
our daily lives.

The Breaking of the Bread

In the Lord's encounter with the disciples, he was not
recognized by them until he broke the bread, a biblical
expression for the celebration of the Eucharist. It was in
the Eucharistic celebration that the disciples knew the
Lord was with them. This experience in Emmaus is an
instruction and reminder to us that the Lord is among
us. As we celebrate the Eucharist as a community of faith,
the Lord is known to us and is present in our lives. We
have to allow ourselves to see and recognize the Lord.
The Eucharistic disclosure is the summit and source of
our entire knowledge of the Lord Jesus. All of our efforts
to be with him, to exercise virtue and learn how to pray,
all of our workings to grow in his grace, always depend
on and flow from his presence in the Eucharist.

Knowing that the Lord is present in the Eucharist, we
should seek to take advantage of opportunities to adore
him, whether that is in Solemn Exposition, Eucharistic
visits during the day, or even in an act of Spiritual
Communion:

My Jesus, I believe that you are present in the most
Blessed Sacrament. I love you above all things and
I desire to receive you into my soul. Since I cannot now receive you sacramentally, come at least
spiritually into my heart. I embrace you as if you
have already come, and unite myself wholly to you.
Never permit me to be separated from you. Amen.

Sacrifice of the Mass

As we celebrate the "breaking of the bread" like the disciples in Emmaus, we are able to be with the Lord, to
participate in the re-representation of his sacrifice to the
Father by the power of the Holy Spirit. Our participation in this sacrifice is a privilege of our Baptism. The
Lord offered his one, historical sacrifice over two thousand years ago, but since the victim was God himself, the
sacrifice continues in time until the Lord returns in glory.
When we go to Mass, we participate in that sacrifice.

An example might help: the internet is running right
now, but perhaps we are not on the internet. Later we
might check our e-mail or go online, and then we click
onto the internet. In a similar way, the Lord's sacrifice is
running right now throughout time, and when we go to
Mass we "click onto" the sacrifice and are sacramentally
present at Calvary with Mary and John the Apostle.

As we "click on" and participate in the Lord's sacrifice, we are able to offer our own lives, our joys and sufferings, to the Father in Jesus Christ. If we attempted to
offer ourselves to God without Jesus Christ, the offering

would be offensive to God's majesty and all-holiness. We offer ourselves, our work, our strengths and weaknesses to the Father in Jesus Christ. This kind of offering only happens in the Eucharist, in the Mass. Through our offering in Jesus Christ, we find a new spirit that enlivens and rejuvenates us in our efforts to see and love the Lord in our daily lives.[66]

Community and Evangelization

After the disciples recognized the Lord, they ran back to Jerusalem. Earlier, they asked the Lord to stay because it was evening and getting dark, but they did not care about that after the Eucharistic disclosure by the Lord Jesus. The two disciples ran back to the Holy City and proclaimed to the community of faith that they had seen the Lord. These disciples are a great example to us of community and evangelization:

- The disciples ran back because they wanted to be in the community of faith. The two realized that believing needs belonging. This is an important lesson for us as we draw closer to the Lord Jesus. We need a community. Sometimes we want to be individuals and stand "on our own two feet," but the way of faith humbles us and calls us to a community where we all stand together. As Christians we need to work on this

---

66   *Catechism of the Catholic Church*, #1324, 1366-1369.

important expression of our discipleship. This is the reason why Bible studies, prayer groups, men's or women's groups, and other such groups are important and helpful to us in our relationship with the Lord. As Christians, we need each other. We are not individuals of faith, but a community of faith.

- The disciples were also great evangelizers. They did not encounter the Lord and then resolve to keep it a secret or mention it discreetly. They ran back to Jerusalem and proclaimed what they had seen and experienced. This is a challenging witness to us. Our culture has privatized religion and taught us not to share or assert any religious beliefs in public. At times, we are uncomfortable with sharing our faith and living our discipleship in public. Our witness, however, is sorely needed in our world. It is also needed in the community of faith. The importance of "faith sharing" among Christians is essential. Such faith sharing does not have to be an indulgence in emotion or border on a superficial expression. It can be virile and mature, as well as extremely edifying and inspiring within the community of faith and society in general. As the disciples shared their faith, so we are also called to share ours, and to proclaim its truths as they did.

Walking with the Lord

As we hear the story of the two disciples with the Lord in Emmaus, we also want to be with him. We respond to his question, "What do you want me to do for you?" with the heartfelt petition that he show us the way. We ask to live in him and to have our eyes opened so that we can see him in our lives.

CHAPTER EIGHT

Living a Life of Prayer

"Watch and pray."
Matthew 26:41

Doing What the Lord Tells Us

The Lord calls us to be with him and to live in his grace. He asks us, "What do you want me to do for you?" The Lord Jesus shows us what discipleship looks like, especially in the Garden of Gethsemane. In the garden, the Lord's human nature is suffering tremendous spiritual and emotional darkness as he sees his impending passion and death. He is filled with grief and anxiety. He desires to do what the Father asks him, but he is afraid. The Lord Jesus turns to the Father, relies on him, and enters into intense prayer. He sweats blood and opens his heart to the Father as he prays, "Abba, Father, all things are possible to you; remove this chalice from me; yet not what I will, but what you will" (Mk 14:36). In the midst of this whirlwind, the Lord says to the apostles, "Watch and pray" (Mt 26:41). He points us to a life of prayer.

Learning to Pray

Some years ago, I was sent to an institute to learn about non-Christian faith traditions. As a part of each module of the institute, we would attend a worship service of the respective tradition. When our segment on Hinduism concluded, we went to a Hindu temple to observe its various religious customs. I wore my Roman collar as we entered the temple, and an American woman in the temple with a Bible in her hand immediately approached me. I wasn't sure what to expect, but she headed straight toward me with obvious resolution. She seemed agitated and asked me, "Do you know why I'm here?" I wasn't sure how to answer, or even if she was expecting an answer. I responded I did not know, and she told me that she went to her local parish and asked if someone could teach her how to pray. She said no one was able to help her, so she turned to the Hindu temple, and the leaders there had guided her in learning how to pray. It was tragic that the woman could not find a Christian guide to teach her how to pray. The Church has a vast treasury, and each of us should seek to learn its richness.

This story illustrates the importance for us to know our spiritual tradition. The woman's desire and inquiry about prayer was a noble one, and her question is also the question on our hearts as well: How do we learn to pray? Where do we start? What can help us to pray?

Nature of Prayer

In first learning how to pray, we have to begin by understanding the nature of prayer. In particular, we have to realize that we are addressing a God who deeply loves us and wants to be in a relationship with us. Having this comprehension, we should avoid certain mentalities that reflect "pagan prayer." Pagan prayer is when we think we have to convince God to do something good for us. We have to assemble armies and force, manipulate, and intimidate God to do something kind and benevolent for us or a loved one. We have to expose this perspective of pagan prayer. As the Lord Jesus teaches us:

> What father among you, if his son asks for a fish, will instead of a fish give him a serpent; or if he asks for an egg, will give him a scorpion? If you then, who are evil, know how to give good gifts to your children, how much more will the heavenly Father give the Holy Spirit to those who ask him!" (Lk 11:11–13)

In coming to know God's providence and affection for us in greater ways, we are able to find deeper peace in our prayer, realizing that we are speaking to our Father who loves us and will do what is best for us and our world. And so we discern one of the great truths of prayer: we pray not to change God, but to change ourselves. Prayer is about a relationship with God. We pray so that we can understand, accept, and live in peace with God's will, knowing of his goodness and kindness to us.[67]

---

67   Catechism of the Catholic Church, #2566-2567, 2742.

Disbelief in the Power of Prayer

Many people express a desire to be people of prayer. We want to pray. Too often, however, people will immediately follow-up such intentions with the assertion that they are too busy, or things are too hectic, or there just is not enough time. As the spiritual masters teach us: if we are too busy to pray, then we are too busy! We always make time to do what we want to do. There is always time to eat, or watch our favorite television show, stop by a coffee bar we like, and many other examples. We make time for what we want to do. So why do people not pray? Why would we express a desire to pray, but then not make the time?

It can be difficult for us to acknowledge, but if we are going to grow and actually begin to pray, then we have to admit some bad assumptions within us. Most people do not pray because they do not think prayer will make a difference, and they do not believe that prayer can help them. These are hard truths to confess, because they touch the core of our faith, but we are fallen and influenced by our materialistic world.[68] Many people would assert: If there is not empirical evidence that prayer works, then why make time for it? As Christians, how would we answer this challenge? How can we convert this false belief within ourselves and begin to grow into a life of prayer?

---

68   *Catechism of the Catholic Church*, #2725-2728.

Consumer Mentality

In response to this challenge, we have to return to the purpose of prayer, which is to develop a relationship with God. In the Lord's public ministry, when he approached the Samaritan woman at Jacob's well, he asked for something to drink. He expressed his thirst so the woman could see and express her own thirst. The *Catechism of the Catholic Church* teaches:

> It is he [Christ] who first seeks us and asks us for a drink. Jesus thirsts; his asking arises from the depths of God's desire for us. Whether we realize it or not, prayer is the encounter of God's thirst with ours. God thirsts that we may thirst for him.[69]

In seeking prayer for what it truly is, we can then unmask some false views of prayer. We live in a society with a strong mercantile, consumer mentality. If we pray, we expect that God will reward us and grant our petitions. We want to change God, and we mistakenly value our prayer by the things we get and which are bestowed upon us, rather than our intimacy and understanding of God.[70]

Imagine what would happen if we were to apply this perspective to our friendships with other people. If we were to seek a relationship with someone based solely on what they could give us, or on what they would surrender to us, then no true friendship would exist. It would be

---

69   *Catechism of the Catholic Church* #2560
70   *Catechism of the Catholic Church, #2735-2736.*

a business venture. If our entire rapport with supposed friends were based solely on this type of *quid-pro-quo*, then there would be no real relationship. It would be a cold exchange of mutual benefits.

As we struggle with this mentality in our comprehension of prayer, we ask God to purify our understanding and teach us to pray. We want to pray and grow in our knowledge of his love and care for us. Our prayer should not be measured by empirical results nor calculated by favors granted. Our prayer is much more interior and intimate than such limited perspectives. Prayer is about a true relationship with God based on love and trust.

Battle of Prayer

Developing a life of prayer is a battle. We pray as we live, because we live as we pray. As we struggle to live our discipleship, so our quest for a life of prayer will also be a struggle. This should not dishearten us, but rather remind us of the necessary place of the purgative way and of how much we need God's help to be people of prayer. The *Catechism of the Catholic Church* illustrates the battle when it teaches:

> In the battle of prayer we must confront erroneous conceptions of prayer, various currents of thought, and our own experience of failure. We must respond with humility, trust, and perseverance to these temptations which cast doubt on the usefulness or even the possibility of prayer.[71]

---

71   *Catechism of the Catholic Church* #2753.

We see the example of the Lord Jesus in the Garden of Gethsemane. Although his human nature was torn and full of sorrow, the Lord remained steadfast and fought the good fight, preserving his prayer and reliance on God the Father. This is a powerful example for us.

In our spiritual tradition, the example of Jacob wrestling in the desert has always been held up for us as a model of tenacity and perseverance in prayer. Jacob was in exile for many years because he lied and stole his brother's blessing. He was tired and wanted to return home. As he was making the journey home and passing through the desert, he stopped for an evening's rest. An unknown person came to him and began to wrestle with him. The two wrestled in the desert, through the night, and as the dawn was breaking, Jacob asked the person his name. The person did not respond, but disjointed Jacob's thigh, and instead gave Jacob a new name. The person told him that his name was no longer Jacob—meaning "liar"—but was now Israel—meaning "God heals." Then the person, now recognized as God, blessed Jacob at daybreak (Gn 32:22–29). Jacob-Israel called that place Peniel, meaning "face of God," because he saw the face of God and lived.

The story of Jacob wrestling in the desert can be an encouragement to us. Jacob was alone in the desert at night, but he wanted to know God and was not going to run away. He was not going to let go. He held on, and God was able to bless him. In our own desire for prayer, we have to welcome the purgative way and fight the battle of prayer. We do not need sand to have a desert, and

at times the Lord will let us experience the desert, its solitude and darkness. As we pray and hold fast, the Lord is
able to purify, heal, re-name, and bless us just as he did
for Jacob.

The Habit of Prayer

Having this understanding of prayer, we want to know
the practicals for developing a habit and life of prayer. We
have made some daily commitments in our rule of life,
but now we need to know the specifics of prayer. When
should we pray? Where should we pray? What posture
should we have when we pray? In our time of prayerful
meditation, what are we supposed to say or do?

When should we pray?

- When we begin to pray, we should place
  our prayer time alongside an existing habit.
  Since our first task is to develop a habit
  of prayer, we should attach our prayer to
  something that we do every day or at a
  specific time each day. For example, we can
  pray while in the shower, or before we brush
  our teeth, or before or after a meal, etc. By
  placing our prayer within these existing
  habits, we allow our prayer itself to become
  a daily habit. We can imagine how it would
  feel if we did not take a shower or brush our
  teeth. Something would not feel right. In
  the same way, as we establish a daily habit of

prayer, it would not feel right for us to miss
our prayer time.

- It is often asked how long we should pray.
  The simple answer is to start small and then
  broaden and deepen the time of prayer. It is
  a good practice to start with five minutes.
  When this was suggested to a group of college students, one responded, "Five minutes? That's too easy," to which the response
  was, "Great! Then do it!" Five minutes can
  be a great start because it is not too difficult, and it helps to form a regular habit.
  Eventually, as a habit develops, five minutes
  could lead to ten or fifteen, and eventually
  twenty minutes. Any prayer time that goes
  beyond a standard twenty minutes should
  be guided by our state in life and our other
  daily responsibilities.

Where should we pray?

- In trying to find a location for our prayer
  time, we should not exaggerate. In the end,
  the only criterion for the location is that
  we are able to pray there. The location for
  our prayer time should be conducive to
  reflection and conversation with God. The
  Lord Jesus tells us: "But when you pray,
  go into your room and shut the door and
  pray to your Father who is in secret; and

your Father who sees in secret will reward you" (Mt 6:6). Praying in our homes or workplaces is a way to sanctify these areas by allowing God's presence to be acknowledged and his grace dispensed. When we are able, we can also pray in a church and before the Blessed Sacrament, which is always a privileged place for prayer.

What posture should we have when we pray?

- In our prayer time, we should take on the posture that most helps us to pray. If we stand, kneel, sit, prostrate, or lie down, it should assist us in talking to the Lord. We should not kneel if it will distract us and we cannot pray. We should not lie down if we will lose our prayer time and fall asleep. The bodily posture we take should serve and nurture the posture of our hearts as we try to pray and encounter God.

In our time of prayerful meditation, what are we to say or do?

- We must remind ourselves that prayer is part of a relationship. It is not a manualistic process, but an act of love and trust. In our prayer, we should turn to the Holy Spirit and ask for help. As St. Paul writes,

"Likewise the Spirit helps us in our weakness; for we do not know how to pray as we ought, but the Spirit himself intercedes for us with sighs too deep for words" (Rom 8:26).

- What do we say when we are praying? This is always the most pressing question. An easy answer: just complain. Yes, complaining can be a great start to prayer. We all do it, and some of the greatest prayers in the Sacred Scriptures are holy people complaining to God. When we complain, we open our hearts, share our struggles, and are transparent. Sometimes people are hesitant to speak to God in this way, but God is big, he can take it, and he wants to hear from us where we really are (and not in an elementary school mode of false piety). Eventually we can move from just complaining to a broader sharing of our lives. We can imagine a conversation we would have with a close friend, and then repeat that conversation to God. This is reaching a deeper intimacy with God. Eventually, as we talk to God as a friend, we can pause and leave time for God to talk to us and for us to hear him.

- In our prayer time with the Lord, the acronym A.C.T.S. might help us. As we talk with

God, we can try to Adore, make Contrition, give Thanks, and offer Supplications for ourselves and others.[72] This acronym is meant as a resource to help us relax and foster a conversation between ourselves and God.

- As we grow in our life of prayer, certain prayer forms within the life of the Church might also be of help to us. There is the "composition of place," in which we use our spiritual imagination to create a biblical scene and place ourselves within it in order to talk with the Lord Jesus. There is *lectio divina*, in which we rhythmically meditate on a specific verse of the Sacred Scriptures and ask the Lord for a word or image to help us. And, there is the *poustinia*, in which we seek to clear all images and thoughts from our mind and sit quietly with God, and ask for a word to teach and direct us. These are only three of many prayer forms in the life of the Church. A good spiritual director will be able to assist us in learning these prayer forms or discovering other ones that will help us to grow in our life of prayer.

- As we review this practical counsel and seek

---

72   *Catechism of the Catholic Church*, #2626-2642.

to fulfill our resolutions concerning prayer, it is extremely helpful if we set self-penances for when we do not observe our prayer time. This is especially important when we are beginning our prayer life and perseverance can be inconsistent. Self-penances should take away something we enjoy (e.g., watching a favorite television show, going to the gym, eating a certain dessert, spending time on social media, etc.). Our self-penance is meant to discipline us so that we remain faithful to our time of prayer.

Following the above counsel will help us to keep our prayer time and assist us in drawing closer to the Lord.

Watch and Pray

The Lord Jesus repeats his question to us: "What do you want me to do for you?" As we see his example of watching and praying, of drawing close to the Father and fulfilling what is asked of him, we reply to the Lord that we want him to show us the way and help us to be with him in prayer. We ask him to help us watch and pray.

CHAPTER NINE

A Prayerful Spirit

"Pray constantly."
1 Thessalonians 5:17

The Thessalonians

The Lord Jesus invites us to pray. He approaches us and asks us again: "What do you want . . ." This was the same question St. Paul asked the Thessalonians. He asked them what they wanted, then he preached the Gospel and they accepted the Lord. St. Paul taught them how to live as Christians. As he left their city, he prayed for them. In perhaps his very first letter, written in the early 50s AD, St. Paul is encouraging the Thessalonians and seeking to sustain the faith of the early community by reminding them of many truths, especially to "pray constantly."

Call to Prayer and Holiness

Each of us is called to be with the Lord and seek holiness in our everyday lives. Along with the Thessalonians, we are told to "pray constantly." This raises questions within us: How can we pray constantly? Does he mean actual formal prayer? If not, what does it mean to pray constantly?

The summons for us to pray constantly does not mean that we are expected to be in formal prayer all the time. It does, however, mean that we should retain a peaceful and prayerful spirit throughout the day. Our formal time of prayer should inspire and sustain us in our everyday tasks and duties. We are called to see God's presence in our responsibilities and to offer them to the Father in Jesus Christ. All that we do, whatever we do, we should do for the glory of God. As St. Paul writes elsewhere:

> So, whether you eat or drink or whatever you do, do all to the glory of God. (1 Cor 10:31)

With this invitation and summons, we should offer God our work, meals, recreation, chores, family life, friendships, as well as our finances, mercy, kindness, sexuality, our political decisions and votes, our joys and sufferings, and all that we do in our lives. Again, St. Paul writes:

> I appeal to you therefore, brethren, by the mercies of God, to present your bodies as a living sacrifice, holy and acceptable to God, which is your spiritual worship. Do not be conformed to this world but be transformed by the renewal of your mind, that you may prove what is the will of God, what is good and acceptable and perfect. (Rom 12:1–2)

Liturgy of the Hours

As we seek to pray constantly, one tremendous gift given to us by the Church is the Liturgy of the Hours. A version of this particular prayer form goes back to the time of King David and the Temple of Solomon. It is a cyclic praying of the Psalms, along with brief readings and revered canticles of the New Testament. The Liturgy of the Hours helps us to focus on the Lord since praying it is meant to prepare us for the Eucharist or prolong its effects in our soul throughout the day. There are seven "hours," which is the formal term used for a designated prayer time, that usually last about ten to fifteen minutes. These seven "hours" are usually observed every three hours throughout the day (excluding midnight). Morning Prayer (called Lauds) and Evening Prayer (called Vespers) are known as the "hinge hours" since they are the main hours that open and close the day's work. The Liturgy of the Hours is binding for those in Holy Orders and in religious life, although all the members of the Church are encouraged to pray it, especially the hinge hours. This is a great resource for all as we want to pray constantly and preserve a spirit of prayerfulness throughout our day.

Solitude and Solidarity

As we look for ways to grow in praying constantly, two areas need to be emphasized: solitude and solidarity. We need to locate and hold onto times in which we can be alone with God. We have to concurrently look for times that involve some type of fellowship with other Christians. Both are needed. According to our personalities, we will be attracted more to one than the other, but we have to stretch ourselves and grow into being comfortable with both solitude and solidarity. Imagine a wife and mother of several children who insists on taking a short walk every day in order to have some solitude for prayer. Or imagine an introverted man who joins his local parish's men's group because he knows that his prayer life needs solidarity with others. These are the sorts of efforts we are called to make in order to live a life of prayer as Christian disciples.

Spiritual Direction

In our pursuit to follow the Lord Jesus and to foster a prayerful spirit throughout the day, the presence and counsel of a spiritual director is a necessity. While the frequency in which we meet with our director can fluctuate, a director's supervision and blessing can be a tremendous affirmation to our efforts to grow in our discipleship. In charity to our director, it is important that we pray for him, prepare well for our sessions, always preserve a transparency and sincerity with him, and that we listen and follow his instructions.

Some important distinctions need to be made in reference to confession, spiritual direction, and pastoral counseling.

Confession is for the admission of sin, repentance, absolution, and healing. The sacrament should not take long. Some signs of maturity in the penitent include: not seeking to explain occasions for sins, readily accusing oneself of our sins, and confessing mortal sins first. Confession is not the occasion for spiritual direction or pastoral counseling. Our spiritual director does not necessarily have to be our confessor. Some people prefer a separate person, and when our director is not a priest (a deacon, religious, or trained lay person) then a priest confessor is needed. If our confessor is different from our spiritual director, then it is advisable that we have a regular confessor and not bounce among priests, etc.

Spiritual direction is for the assessment of our discipleship. This is the cherished forum in which we can discuss the causes of our sin, our struggle with prayer, etc. Our rule of life is a great agenda for our sessions with a spiritual director. Spiritual direction is not the proper occasion for pastoral counseling. If pastoral counseling is needed, then we should conclude our formal session of spiritual direction, and then ask our director for pastoral counseling on an issue.

Pastoral counseling is when we seek guidance from a priest (or a fellow believer trained in this area) on an issue in our lives that is causing us unrest or great concern, and we wish to be counseled on how to address the issue in the light of faith. Pastoral counseling is distinct from clinical counseling in that its focus is solely to assist a believer in applying the truths of faith to issues in their life.

An example might help: If we were to show a lack of charity to a family member, then we would go to confession for absolution and healing from this sin, then perhaps to spiritual direction to discern the root cause of our lack of charity and spiritual means to temper and conquer it, and then perhaps to pastoral counseling to address our history and problems with this particular family member.

Each of these three resources is given to us as a help in our discipleship with the Lord Jesus. In particular, spiritual direction is a great means for us to explore and deepen our relationship with Christ and to constantly live a spirit of prayer.

General Examen

In seeking to pray constantly, a great means for us in our daily lives is the examen prayer. The word "examen" is Spanish for "examination." There are two types of examens: the particular examen and the general examen. We have already discussed the particular exam (reform of life) in the presentation on the rule of life. So we now have to try and understand the general examen: What is this general examen? How is it done? How can it help us?

The general examen is a broad review of our day or part of our day. It seeks to identify the presence of God, discern his will, and seek amendment for any faults. Traditionally, there are five steps in the general examen. These have been piously associated with the five wounds of Christ, which illustrates how the general examen can help us to see the Lord Jesus and apply his redemption in our daily lives.

It is recommended that the general examen be done in the afternoon and evening, or only in the evening. It can be done on our lunch break, on the drive home from work, or in our beds before going to sleep, etc. The examen begins with the Lord's Prayer. This is meant to help us transition to a state of prayer. Once there, the general examen begins:

- Presence. We acknowledge God's presence in our lives and in our day. We try to identify any specific occasions that manifested his presence to us.

- Gratitude. We thank God for his blessings upon us. We attempt to name some of those blessings.

- Examination. We go through our day chronologically and try to identify times or ways in which we committed sin by commission or omission. We can apply aspects of our particular examen by looking for manifestations of our dominant defect.

- Mercy. We repent of our sins and ask the Lord for his pardon and peace.

- Resolution. We make a clear and practical resolution for the later part of our day, or for the following day, that will help God's grace to work and amend our weaknesses and offenses against God or our neighbor.

The general examen is a practical resource for us as we seek to pray constantly.

Unitive Way

In our discipleship, there are three ways, or stages, in which we can grow in our intimacy with God. We have already addressed the purgative way and the illuminative way. As we deepen in our life of virtue and prayer, God may choose to lead us to the unitive way. Although we all have the grace for the unitive way through Baptism, the spiritual masters assert that very few of us will attain this way in our life on earth. The unitive way is when we are completely united to God, we move from quiet contemplation to contemplative absorption. This is when God is fully praying through us. In this way of the spiritual life, we go through two tremendous "nights": the dark night of the senses and the dark night of the soul. Many times, people will falsely associate the darkness of the purgative way with these nights of the unitive way. We must be careful not to confuse these different aspects of the spiritual life. The dark nights are passages for a person in the unitive way to enter starkly and with no consolation of the senses or the spiritual powers into God and live completely in him. While it is good for us to know of this way of the spiritual life, we should stay focused on our particular spiritual work at hand. The unitive way is a gift from God and is given as he wills.

Praying Constantly

As we present these different parts of our discipleship, we hear the Lord ask us: "What do you want me to do for you?" We ask him to show us the way and to teach us how to pray constantly. We want to be holy, to be with him in all that we do, say, and think.

Conclusion

Some time ago, a young college student expressed great interest in becoming a Catholic Christian. He was raised in a devout Protestant family and was formed in a strong relationship with the Lord. As his interest in Catholicism grew, and he found so many answers to his questions, he began to pine for the fullness of the Christian faith. Eventually, he asked a priest if he would come and meet with his parents. The priest was expecting the usual round of questions about the pope, Mary, the Eucharist, purgatory, etc., but none of these questions even came up. Instead, the parents asked the priest multiple questions about discipleship. They were concerned that their son's conversion to Catholicism would hurt or weaken his discipleship. They asked the priest about prayer, studies of the Sacred Scriptures, the moral life of Catholics, and an array of similar questions. The priest was amazed and edified by the questions.

These have been our questions, too, and in the course of our book we have sought to answer them and walk through three principal parts of our discipleship. Each part has led us into a new and deeper relationship with the Lord.

In Part One, Jesus Christ as "Lord" was addressed. The need for a life of faith and discipleship was displayed, and we were guided by the Lord's question: "Who do you say that I am?" (Mt 16:15) The identity of Jesus Christ and Baptism was explored, and our need for a personal relationship with him was emphasized. The central place of the Eucharist was addressed, and the Church as a community of faith was explained.

In Part Two, our petition to the Lord Jesus to "Teach Us" was covered. The important aspects of conversion and virtue in the life of a Christian disciple were stressed. Guided by the Lord's question: "Why do you call me 'Lord, Lord,' and not do what I tell you?" (Lk 6:46), explained the purgative way, God's law, virtue, and the Rule of Life.

In Part Three our request of the Lord to teach us how "To Pray" was developed. The universal call to holiness and the different understandings of prayer were highlighted. The Lord's question: "What do you want me to do for you?" (Lk 18:41) served as a guide. In the encounter with this question, the Eucharist was shown as the summit and source of our way of life. Practical counsel was given on how to begin or deepen our time of prayer, how to persevere in prayer, and how to sanctify our daily activities in Jesus Christ.

As we have walked with the Lord Jesus through the lessons of our book, we return to our original petition, "Lord, teach us to pray," and we now have three questions given to us:

- "Who do you say that I am?"

- "Why do you call me 'Lord, Lord,' and not do what I tell you?"

- "What do you want me to do for you?"

In receiving the Lord's goodness, and having sat at his feet and received his teaching, we are now able to respond:

- "Who do you say that I am?"
- **"LORD"**
- "Why do you call me 'Lord, Lord,' and not do what I tell you?"
- **"TEACH US"**
- "What do you want me to do for you?"
- **Teach us "TO PRAY"**

We are able to give our answers because the Lord has become our friend, teacher, healer, confidante, and companion. We are able to answer because the Lord Jesus has become the Answer in our lives. The Lord calls us, loves us, forms us, and now sends us in his Name.

Bibliography

Anonymous, *Thirty Favorite Novenas*, Charlotte, NC: TAN Books, 2009.

_____, *A Year with the Saints: A Virtue for Every Month of the Year*, Charlotte, NC: TAN Books, 2009.

Aumann, Jordan, *Christian Spirituality in the Catholic Tradition*, San Francisco, CA: Ignatius Press., 1985

_____ *Spiritual Theology*. London: Continuum Press, 1980.

Barron, Robert, *And Now I See...:A Theology of Transformation*, New York: The Crossroad Publishing Company, 1999..

Benedict XVI, Pope, *God is Love*, 2005.

Benedictine Sisters of Perpetual Adoration, *Seven Capital Sins*, TAN Books, 2009.

Bible, Revised Standard Version (Catholic Edition), Charlotte, NC: TAN Books, 2009.

Catechism of the Catholic Church

de Caussade, Fr. Jean Pierre, *Abandonment to Divine Providence*, Charlotte, NC: TAN Books, 2010

Chautard, Fr. Jean-Baptiste, *The Soul of the Apostolate*, Charlotte, NC: TAN Books

Dubay, Thomas, *Fire Within*. Ignatius Press

Garrigou-Lagrange, Reginald, *The Three Conversions in the Spiritual Life*. TAN Books

Groeschel, Benedict, *Spiritual Passages: The Psychology of Spiritual Development*, New York: The Crossroad Publishing Company, 1984.

John Paul II, Pope, *Redeemer of Man*, 1979.

_____, *Mission of the Redeemer*, 1990.

_____ *Splendor of Truth*, 1993.

Kempis, Thomas, *The Imitation of Christ*, Charlotte, NC: TAN Books, 2010.

Laux, Fr. John *Introduction to the Bible*, Charlotte, NC: TAN Books, 2009.

Lewis, C.S., *Mere Christianity*, San Francisco, CA: Harper, 2009.

Manning, Cardinal Henry Edward, *Sin and its Consequences*, Charlotte, NC: TAN Books, 2009.

McElhone, James, *Particular Examen*. Roman Catholic Books, 1952.

Nelson, Thomas A., *Catholic Prayers*, Charlotte, NC: TAN Books, 2010.

Philippe, Jacques, *Time for God*, New Rochelle, NY: Scepter Publishers, 2008.

Pinckaers, Servais, *The Sources of Christian Ethics,* Washinton, DC: Catholic University of America Press, 1995.

Richard, R. Thomas, *The Ordinary Path to Holiness,* Staten Island, NY: Alba House, 2002.

St. Louis de Montfort, *True Devotion to Mary,* Charlotte, NC: TAN Books, 2010.

St. Therese of Lisieux, *The Story of a Soul,* Charlotte, NC: TAN Books, 2010.

About the Author

Fr. Jeff Kirby is a priest of the Diocese of Charleston. He holds a Licentiate in Moral Theology from the Holy Cross University in Rome. As the diocesan Vicar of Vocations for the past several years, Fr. Kirby has guided numerous young men and women in the spiritual life and in the process of discernment. In 2011, he founded the Drexel House, a Catholic Residence for Men.